KETO DIET INSTANT POT COOKBOOK
1000 DAY KETO DIET FOR BEGINENRS

Copyright 2018 by World Good Foods Ltd   ISBN: 978-1-9997873-4-9
www.worldgoodfoods.com

The recipes and information in this book are provided for educational purposes only. Everyone needs are different, and these recipes and methods reflect specifically on what has worked for the author. This book is not intended to provide medical advice or take the place of medical treatment from qualified health care professionals. All readers who are taking any form of prescription medication should consult with their physicians before making any changes to their current eating habits. Neither the publisher nor the author takes any responsibility for any possible consequences of any person reading or following the information in this book.

Table of Contents

Getting Started — 3

Chicken
Chicken Hainanese — 4
Poached Chicken in Coconut & Lime Cream Sauce — 5
Tamarind & Lemongrass Braised Chicken — 6
Roasted Tandoori Chicken — 7
Chicken Shawarma with Spicy Orange Sauce — 8
Healthy Chicken Cacciatore — 9
Stuffed Chicken — 10

Turkey
Juniper and Citrus Turkey Leg Confit — 11
Stuffed Turkey Thighs — 12
Ground Turkey Stir Fry — 13
Glazed Turkey Wings — 14

Pork
Scrumptious Pork Chili — 15
Pork Luau — 16
Deonjang Pork Spare Ribs — 17
Jamaican Jerk Pork Roast — 18
Avocado & Bacon Stuffed Peppers — 19
Tuscan Herbed Pork Chops — 20

Soups & Stews
Minted Cream Soup — 21
Asparagus and Celery Soup — 22
Chicken & Vegetable Soup — 23
Spinach Chipotle Soup — 24
Spicy Beef Cauliflower Soup — 25
Crab & Winter Bamboo Shoot Egg Drop Soup — 26
Hearty Keto Beef Stew — 27

Lamb
Spicy Masala Lamb Chops — 28
Port Wine Lamb Shanks — 29
Grilled Lamb & Veggies Bowl — 30
Lamb Leg with Gravy — 31
Lamb Ribs — 32
Luscious Lamb Skewers — 33

Beef
Balsamic & Rosemary Roast Beef — 34
Oatmeal Beef Meatballs — 35
Scrumptious Italian Beef with Avocado — 36
Ground Beef Skewers — 37

Fish & Seafood
Sweet Peppercorn Salmon — 38
Seafood Medley Stew — 39
Lemon Kalamata Olive Salmon — 40
Creamy Chile Shrimp — 41
Baked Cod — 42

Vegetarian
Vegetable Hash — 43
Egg Frittata — 44
Scrambled Tofu — 45
Coconut Cabbage — 46
Crispy Feta with Zucchini Ribbons — 47
Green Wraps — 48
Savoury Cauliflower Patties — 49

Dessert
Chocolate Pudding — 50
Tangy Berry Slice — 51
Fluffy Eggy Muffins — 52
Spiced Gluten-Free Pancakes — 53
Peanut Butter Cheesecake — 54
Almond Carrot Cake — 55

Recipe & Snack Nutrional Values — 56

Keto Meal Plan Schedules — 58

Getting Started

First, I would like to thank you for purchasing this book. I hope it helps you reaching your health and wellness goals and that you enjoy preparing the dishes I have created. Following the ketogenic diet is quite straightforward and these recipes are meant to be simple but packed with flavour so you have plenty of fun cooking them while following your keto diet journey. At the end of the book you will find a combination of schedules for different dietary needs making up 1000 days of Keto daily eating plans.

How to use this information?

I recommend using the calorie & macro calculator below. This will allow you to customize your diet to your needs without complication:
http://bit.ly/CalculateMacros

How do I select my recipes?

In this book you will find a variety of ketogenic recipes with their calories, fat, protein and carbs per serving detailed. Many recipes display two versions: Low fat and high fat, each one with their different dietary information listed.

Before preparing a recipe, you must decide what version to cook, and this will depend on your personal requirements. Recipes list "common ingredients" which are the same for both versions, and then "Low fat version" and "High fat version" ingredients. Some recipes have only one version though.

To make things easier, at the end of this book, there is a summary with all the nutritional information for all the recipes, so you can have a quick look and select which ones match your requirements, presenting the correct numbers for your individual needs. Also, there are snacks included.

After the recipe summary, I have introduced a few examples of eating schedules for a variety or dietary needs. I hope you find these useful.

First step

Simply input your age, height, weight, gender, current exercise activity levels, body fat and weight goals (the goals are fixed to weight loss by default). Initially, leave carbs at the default amount. These will be adjusted on your last step.

Not always people know their body fat percentage. To assist you with this, I have provided you with theWorld Good Foods body fat calculator here:
http://bit.ly/CalculateBodyFatPercentage

Second Step

You may choose to calculate your body fat % the simplified way by selecting "Without any Tool". Selecting "Tape" and a calculation sub-method will allow you to define a more tailored result. You will just need measuring your wrist, hips, waist, forearm, etc.

Third Step

Once you input your body fat % in the keto calculator, a list of 3 tables with macros will appear below. You must choose the one adhering the most to your dieting expectations, choosing one of the recommended calorie deficits.

Final Step

Check the target number of calories in your chosen table. Get this number divided by 80, scroll up and input the result on the "Carbs" option. This will force carbs down to just 5% of your calories (Remember, Keto diets are very low in carbs). Once you do this, scroll back down to your table.

Now write down your calories, fat, protein and carb targets. With these data you will be able to pick and choose recipes hitting your required targets. Also, you may choose one of our schedules at the end of the book. Choose the one that fits the most to your dietary needs.

Chicken Hainanese

Ingredients

Common Ingredients

- 1 Oz (25g.) Ginger, peeled
- 6 cloves Garlic, crushed
- 6 x bundles of Pandan Leaves/cilantro/Thai basil
- 1 tsp. Salt
- 1/3 cup Sesame Oil

For the ginger dip (common)

- 2 tbsp. minced Ginger
- 1 tsp. minced Garlic
- 1 tbsp. Chicken Stock
- 1 tsp. Sesame Oil
- ½ tsp. Sugar

Low fat version ingredients

- 3 x 1/2lb (3x225g.) ready to cook yield Chicken (no skin)

High fat version ingredients

- 3 x 1/2lb (3x225g.) ready to cook yield Chicken (meat and skin)

Nutrition

Prep: 20 min **Cook:** 4h **Serves:** 3

High Fat Version
- Kcal per serve: 535
- Fat: 45 g. (75%)
- Protein: 28 g. (21%)
- Carbs: 5 g (4%)

Low Fat Version
- Kcal per serve: 351
- Fat: 27 g. (68%)
- Protein: 22 g. (26%)
- Carbs: 5 g (6%)

Flavorful and fragrant, this chicken is easily poached to perfection. A Hainan original made simple in your Instant-Pot!

Tip: If you can't find Pandan leaves locally, feel free to replace it by Basil or Cilantro.

Preparation

1. Combine chicken, garlic, ginger, Pandan leaves, and salt in the pot.
2. Add enough water to fully submerge the chicken and cook on slow cooker mode set low for 4 hours. Let pressure release naturally.
3. Carefully take the chicken out of the pot and chill in a bowl of iced water for 10 minutes.
4. Meanwhile, combine all ingredients for the ginger dip in a food processor and pulse into a coarse paste.
5. Take the chicken out of the ice bath, drain, and chop into serving pieces. Arrange onto a serving platter and brush with sesame oil. Serve the chicken with ginger dip on the side.

Poached Chicken in Coconut & Lime Cream Sauce

Nutrition

Prep: 5 min **Cook:** 10 min **Serves:** 4

High Fat Version	Low Fat Version
Kcal per serve: 429	**Kcal** per serve: 300
Fat: 33 g. (68%)	**Fat:** 20 g. (58%)
Protein: 24 g. (24%)	**Protein:** 21 g. (30%)
Carbs: 9 g (8%)	**Carbs:** 9 g (12%)

Perfectly moist chicken pieces in a creamy coconut and lime poaching sauce. Creamy and tangy, rich yet light, spicy and cool at the same time. Asian cuisine has its wonders…

Ingredients

Common Ingredients

- 1 Oz (25g.) Shallot, minced
- 1 Oz (25g.) Ginger, thinly sliced
- 1 ½ medium Banana Peppers
- 1/2 cup Coconut milk
- 1 cup Chicken stock
- Juice and zest of 1 Lime
- 2 tablespoon Fish Sauce
- 1/2 Cup of peeled walnuts
- Cilantro, for garnish

Low fat version ingredients

- 3 x 1/3lb (3x150g.) Chicken (ready to cook yield, no skin)

High fat version ingredients

- 3 x 1/3lb (3x150g.) Chicken (ready to cook yield, meat and skin)

Preparation

1. Combine all the ingredients inside the pot.
2. Cook on high pressure for 10 minutes. Quick release pressure.
3. Top with fresh cilantro.

Chicken 5

Tamarind & Lemongrass Braised Chicken

NUTRITION

Prep: 10 min   **Cook:** 4h   **Serves:** 4

Kcal per serve: 445   **Protein:** 28 g. (26%)
Fat: 32 g. (66%)   **Carbs:** 9 g (8%)

Rendering a deep-flavored chicken broth creates truly rewarding results. Add the fruity tang of tamarind, the citrusy notes of lemongrass, and the soothing warmth of turmeric and you've got a dish every bit worthy of being classified as comfort food.

Tip: Ginger can be substituted for turmeric in a pinch!

INGREDIENTS

- 3 Chicken Thighs, (meat and skin)
- 1/2 stalk Lemongrass, bruised and bundled-up
- 2 tbsp Tamarind Paste or Substitute
- (Substitute: Lime Juice+ Brown Sugar at equal parts)
- 1/2 Oz (15g) strips Fresh Turmeric/Curry or Cumin powder
- 1 1/4 cups Chicken Stock
- 1 Roma Tomatoes, quartered
- Salt to taste
- ½ Oz (15 g) Shallots, quartered
- 1/2 Banana Peppers
- 1/2 Radish, peeled and chopped
- Pepper to taste
- A handful Mustard Leaves/ Kale/Turnip
- 2 tbsp olive oil
- Fish Sauce to taste

PREPARATION

1. Combine all ingredients inside the pot.
2. Cook on slow cooker mode set low for 4 hours. Quick release pressure.
3. Add the mustard leaves and leave to wilt for a few minutes over keep warm setting.

Roasted Tandoori Chicken

Ingredients

6 Pieces Chicken Thighs, (bone-in)
1 tsp. Tandoori Paste
1 tbsp. Lemon Juice
Salt, pepper and lemon juice to taste.

Nutrition

Prep: 5 min   **Cook:** 15 min   **Serves:** 4

Kcal per serve: 675   **Protein**: 49 g. (31%)
Fat: 50 g. (67%)   **Carbs**: 4 g (2%)

Perfectly succulent roasted chicken thighs, flavored in a spiced yogurt mix, then finished off to crisp on a hot grill. Serve this Indian classic for an alternative Sunday barbeque with family and friends.

Preparation

1. Mix yogurt, lemon juice, and tandoori paste in a large bowl.
2. Toss the chicken thighs into the tandoori mixture and marinate overnight.
3. Season the chicken with salt and pepper.
4. Put the chicken, marinade, and half cup of water into the pot. Cook on high pressure for 10 minutes. Let pressure release naturally.
5. Take the chicken thighs out of the Instant Pot and sear for 3 minutes per side on the grill.

Chicken

Chicken Shawarma with Spicy Orange Sauce

Nutrition

Prep: 10 min **Cook:** 15 min **Serves:** 3

High Fat Version
Kcal per serve: 725
Fat: 60 g. (73%)
Protein: 37 g. (22%)
Carbs:- 9 g (5%)

Low Fat Version
Kcal per serve: 645
Fat: 48 g. (66%)
Protein: 44 g. (29%)
Carbs: 9 g (5%)

Don't let the exotic name fool you. This dish is bursting with flavors and will impress your guests for sure!

Tip: Instead of mashed sweet potato, try a medley of sautéed onions, mushrooms and zucchini for a colorful, low starch side!

Ingredients

Common Ingredients
- 3/4 lb.(330g.) chicken breasts (meat & skin)
- 1/8 tsp. cinnamon
- 1/4 tsp. chili powder
- 1 tsp. ground cumin
- 1/4 tsp. ground allspice
- 1/4 tsp. granulated garlic
- 1/2 tsp. turmeric
- 1 tsp. paprika
- Pinch of salt
- Pinch of pepper

For the Sauce (common)
- 1/2 cup chicken broth
- 1 tbs. hot chili sauce
- 2 tbsp. tomato paste
- ½ cup fresh orange juice
- 1 tbsp. chopped chives
- 1/4 cup fresh lemon juice
- 1 tbsp. grated ginger
- 1 tsp salt
- 1 cup water

Low fat version ingredients
- 3/4 lb.(330g.) chicken thighs (meat & skin)
- 4 tbsp. coconut oil

High fat version ingredients
- 1/2 lb.(225g.) chicken thighs (meat & skin)
- 8 tbsp. coconut oil

Preparation

1. Mix all ingredients in your instant pot and lock lid; cook on poultry setting for 15 minutes and then release pressure naturally.

2. Make the sauce: add a teaspoon of olive oil to a skillet and set over medium high heat; sauté grated ginger for 1 minute and then stir in the remaining ingredients, except, hot chili sauce and lemon juice.

3. Serve chicken drizzled with tahini sauce.

Healthy Chicken Cacciatore

NUTRITION

Prep: 10 min **Cook:** 25 min **Serves:** 3

High Fat Version
Kcal per serve: 610
Fat: 50 g. (73%)
Protein: 33 g. (23%)
Carbs: 7 g (4%)

Low Fat Version
Kcal per serve: 600
Fat: 43 g. (65%)
Protein: 44 g. (31%)
Carbs: 7 g (4%)

A high protein diet is essential to sustainable weight loss because it helps to build and maintain muscle mass. Bell peppers, onions and tomatoes are great for boosting metabolism, too.

Tip: Use chicken thighs instead of breasts.

INGREDIENTS

Common Ingredients
1/4 cup diced red bell pepper
1/2 cup diced green bell pepper
1/2 cup diced onion
1 cup crushed tomatoes
1 bay leaf / thyme/ juniper berries
1/2 tsp. dried oregano
salt & pepper
2 tbsp. chopped basil

Low fat version ingredients
4 chicken thighs, skin and meat

High fat version ingredients
3 chicken thighs, skin and meat
¼ cup olive oil

PREPARATION

1. Season chicken with salt and pepper and add to a greased instant pot; set the pot to sauté mode and then cook chicken until browned on both sides. Transfer to a platter and set aside.

2. Add more oil to the pot and cook peppers and onion until tender; stir in tomatoes, chicken, veggies, bay leaf, oregano, salt and pepper and lock lid. Cook on high for 25 minutes; let pressure come down naturally and then discard bay leaf.

Chicken 9

Stuffed Chicken

INGREDIENTS

Common Ingredients
- 2 tbsp. Lemon Juice
- 1 tbsp. Garlic Powder
- 1 tsp. Paprika Powder
- ½ tbsp. Mustard Powder
- 2 tbsp. Lemon Juice

For the Stuffing (common)
- ½ cup Shredded Mozzarella Cheese
- ½ cup Pitted Black Olives

Low fat version ingredients
- 1 lb. (450g.) Boneless Chicken Breasts
- 3 tbsp. Olive Oil

For the Stuffing (low fat)
- 4 tbsp. Butter

High fat version ingredients
- ¾ lb. (330g.) Boneless Chicken Breasts
- 4 tbsp. Olive Oil

For the Stuffing (high fat)
- ½ cup Shredded Cheddar Cheese
- 5 tbsp. Butter

NUTRITION

Prep: 8 h   **Cook:** 25 min   **Serves:** 3

High Fat Version
- **Kcal** per serve: 615
- **Fat**: 50 g. (72%)
- **Protein**: 36 g. (24%)
- **Carbs**: 5 g (3%)

Low Fat Version
- **Kcal** per serve: 545
- **Fat**: 40 g. (66%)
- **Protein**: 39 g. (30%)
- **Carbs**: 5 g (4%)

This recipe has a great Mediterranean flair to it and is easy to put together on a busy night!

Tip: If using frozen chicken breasts, thaw completely before preparation. Replace black olives with green for a nuttier flavor. Toss fresh leafy greens with lemon juice and olive oil for a delicious complement to the dish.

PREPARATION

1. In a bowl, mix lemon juice, garlic powder, paprika and mustard powder.
2. Slit each chicken breast from the middle carefully.
3. Rub the marinade on the chicken breasts and refrigerate for 2-4 hours at least.
4. Mix the cheese, olives and butter and stuff each breast with this mixture. Seal the breasts with toothpicks.
5. Put olive oil in the pot and sauté chicken breasts (2 at a time) for 3-4 minutes each side.
6. Remove chicken breasts. Put 1 cup of water and place chicken on the trivet in the pot. Cook for 8 minutes. Release pressure naturally. Take the chicken breasts out of the Instant Pot, remove toothpicks and serve.

Juniper and Citrus Turkey Leg Confit

INGREDIENTS

Common Ingredients
- 8 Juniper Berries
- 1/4 tsp Gin
- Zest of 1 Orange
- Zest of 2 Lemons
- 1 tbsp Black or White Peppercorns/White pepper
- 2 tbsp Coarse Salt

Low fat version ingredients
- 3 Turkey Drumsticks (4oz, no bone yield, meat only)
- 3 tbsp Olive Oil

High fat version ingredients
- 3 Turkey Drumsticks (4oz, no bone yield, meat and skin)
- 6 tbsp Olive Oil

NUTRITION

Prep: 8h   Cook: 5 h   Serves: 2

High Fat Version
- Kcal per serve: 640
- Fat: 53 g. (75%)
- Protein: 35 g. (20%)
- Carbs: 5 g (3%)

Low Fat Version
- Kcal per serve: 405
- Fat: 27 g. (60%)
- Protein: 35 g. (35%)
- Carbs: 5 g (4%)

Use super flavorful dark turkey leg meat, with a fresh aromatic blend of juniper berries and orange zest.

Tip: Getting the turkey legs completely submerged in olive oil is key to making this confit. Add some sprigs of fresh herb into the pot for more aroma. Tarragon and rosemary would be excellent choices.

PREPARATION

1. Combine all ingredients in a bowl and leave to marinate overnight.
2. Transfer turkey drumsticks and marinade into the pot.
3. Set pot to slow cooker mode on low and leave for 4 hours. Leave to release pressure naturally.
4. Carefully take the turkey legs out of the pot and transfer to a baking sheet.
5. Roast in the oven for 15-20 minutes at 350F.

Turkey

Stuffed Turkey Thighs

INGREDIENTS

Common Ingredients
- 1 cup (200 ml) Chicken Broth
- 2 tbsp. (30 ml) Lemon Juice
- ½ tsp. (2.5 g.) Thyme & Rosemary
- ½ cup (100 ml) Heavy Cream (Fluid)
- ¾ cup (150 g.) Bell Pepper, chopped
- 2 tbsp. (30 g.) Crushed Garlic
- ½ cup (100 g.) Zucchinis, diced
- Salt and pepper to taste

Low fat version ingredients
- 2 lbs. (900 g.) Turkey Thighs
- 2 tbsp. (30 g.) Light Butter

High fat version ingredients
- 1 1/4 lbs. (560 g.) Turkey Thighs
- 3 tbsp. (45 g.) Unsalted Butter
- 4 tbsp. (60 ml.) Canola Oil
- ½ cup (100 g.) Feta Cheese

NUTRITION

Prep: 20 min **Cook:** 30 min **Serves:** 4

High Fat Version
- **Kcal** per serve: 568
- **Fat:** 47 g. (73%)
- **Protein:** 33 g. (24%)
- **Carbs:** 5 g (3%)

Low Fat Version
- **Kcal** per serve: 585
- **Fat:** 42 g. (63%)
- **Protein:** 46 g. (33%)
- **Carbs:** 6 g (4%)

Not only are these totally keto, but they are easy to prepare and elegant looking when served.

Tip: Make sure you are evenly flattening your turkey pieces so they cook evenly.

PREPARATION

1. Place turkey thighs between sheets of plastic wrap. Pound with a meat hammer until uniformly spread out and about half inch thick.

2. Put butter and zucchini inside Instant Pot and cook on high pressure for 5 minutes. Release pressure naturally. Remove zucchini and add in oil, garlic and bell pepper. Sautee until peppers are soft.

3. Let the vegetables cool, then mix with crumbled feta cheese

4. Rub lemon juice, herbs, salt and pepper on the turkey fillets.

5. Place stuffing on the fillet and tightly roll. Secure with cooking twine. Sauté stuffed fillets until browned on both sides.

6. Put 1 cup of chicken broth in the Instant Pot and place the stuffed thighs in a baking pan on the trivet. Cook on high pressure for 20 minutes. Quick release pressure.

Ground Turkey Stir Fry

INGREDIENTS

Common Ingredients
6 cups (500 g.) Chinese Cabbage
1 tbsp. (15 g.) Minced Garlic
1 tbsp. (15 ml) Rice Vinegar
½ tsp. (2.5 g) Minced Ginger
Salt and pepper to taste

Low fat version ingredients
1½ lbs. (680 g.) Ground Turkey (93% Lean)
¼ cup (50 ml) Olive Oil

High fat version ingredients
1 lbs. (450 g.) Ground Turkey (93% Lean)
½ cup (100 ml) Olive Oil

NUTRITION

Prep: 5 min   **Cook:** 20 min   **Serves:** 3

High Fat Version
Kcal per serve: 590
Fat: 49 g. (75%)
Protein: 30 g. (21%)
Carbs: 7 g (4%)

Low Fat Version
Kcal per serve: 587
Fat: 47 g. (35%)
Protein: 36 g. (61%)
Carbs: 5 g (3%)

An Asian flavor inspired stir fry. All it takes is the Instant Pot, a few ingredients and some hot oil. A midweek dinner comes together within minutes with this recipe.

Tip: This is great served cold!

PREPARATION

1. In the Instant Pot, heat the oil and add ginger and garlic. Sauté until it turns golden brown. Add cabbage to the Pot. Stir fry until the leaves begin to wilt. Remove from Pot.

2. Add ground turkey and cook until it changes color completely.

3. Add vinegar and seasonings. Cook until the turkey is completely done.

Turkey

Glazed Turkey Wings

INGREDIENTS

Common Ingredients
- 1 cup (200 ml) Chicken Broth
- ½ cup (100 ml) Hot Sauce
- 1 tbsp. (15 g.) Almond Flour
- 1 tsp. (5 g.) Paprika
- 1 tsp. (5 g.) Garlic Powder
- ½ tsp. (2.5 g.) Mustard
- Salt and Pepper to taste

Low fat version ingredients
- 1 1/2 lbs. (680g.) Turkey Wings (Without Skin)
- 4 tbsp. (50 ml) Soybean Oil
- 2 tbsp. (30 g.) Sun Dried Tomatoes
- 1 tbsp. (15 ml) Soy Sauce

High fat version ingredients
- 1 lb. (450g.) Turkey Wings (Without Skin)
- 9½ tbsp. (140 ml) Soybean Oil
- 1 tbsp. (15 g.) Sun Dried Tomatoes
- 1 tsp. (5 ml) Soy Sauce

NUTRITION

Prep: 5 min   **Cook:** 35 min   **Serves:** 3

High Fat Version
- **Kcal** per serve: 590
- **Fat:** 47 g. (71%)
- **Protein:** 38 g. (27%)
- **Carbs:** 4 g (3%)

Low Fat Version
- **Kcal** per serve: 470
- **Fat:** 24 g. (45%)
- **Protein:** 56 g. (50%)
- **Carbs:** 6 g (5%)

Tender, juicy turkey wings smothered in a tangy sweet and sour sauce that will tingle your taste buds. This essential game day snack is a breeze to put together.

Tip: Turkey wings are usually meatier than chicken, giving you more cluck for your buck!

PREPARATION

1. In the Instant Pot, heat the oil. Sauté wings in batches until they become brown.
2. Add the rest of the ingredients except almond flour and cook on high pressure for 9 minutes. Quick release pressure.
3. Remove turkey wings from the Pot and place in a baking tray lined with parchment paper. Broil in the oven until the skin is crispy.
4. Meanwhile, let the sauce simmer in the Instant Pot. Add almond flour and keep stirring.
5. When the sauce thickens, add the broiled turkey wings and coat in the sauce.

Scrumptious Pork Chili

NUTRITION

Prep: 10 min **Cook:** 30 min **Serves:** 3

High Fat Version	Low Fat Version
Kcal per serve: 540	**Kcal** per serve: 430
Fat: 43 g. (71%)	**Fat:** 30 g. (63%)
Protein: 30 g. (22%)	**Protein:** 30 g. (28%)
Carbs: 10 g (7%)	**Carbs:** 10 g (9%)

Another game day favorite the entire family will enjoy!

Tip: Substitute peppers for other fresh green chiles. Stir a few tablespoons of salsa in the chili just before serving to add an extra flavor.

INGREDIENTS

Common Ingredients

- 1 lb. (450g.) coarsely ground pork (84% lean and 16% fat)
- 1/2 can diced tomatoes
- 1/2 hot yellow peppers, deseeded and chopped
- ½ tbsp. cacao powder
- ½ tbsp. ancho Chile powder / mild paprika
- 1 Oz. (15g.) arrow root powder
- 1 tbsp. cumin
- 1 tbsp. garlic powder
- 2 tbsp. ground coriander
- 1 tbsp. dried oregano
- ¼ cup low sodium beef broth, preferably homemade

Low fat version ingredients
- 1 tbsp. olive oil

High fat version ingredients
- 4 tbsp. olive oil

PREPARATION

1. Start by browning your pork in a skillet in olive oil, in batches before putting it in your instant pot, draining any excess fat in the process. Once all the pork is in your pot, heat a bit of oil in the same skillet you used to brown the pork and sauté the veggies until tender. Stir in all the seasonings and continue cooking until the skillet dries up.

2. Drain the tomatoes and add them to the skillet. Stir well then transfer all the contents of the skillet to your pot. Do not stir just layer the veggies on top then pour in the broth. Lock lid and cook for 30 minutes; let pressure come down on its own.

3. Mix the arrow root powder with a little water then pour it in the pot together with the cacao powder; cover and let sit for a few minutes before serving. Drop evenly rest of oil if any on the dish.

Pork

Pork Luau

Ingredients

- 2lb.(900g) Pork Shoulder
- 1 tablespoon Coarse Salt
- 2 tablespoons Liquid Smoke (or substitute)
- Substitutes: Spanish smoked paprika or Chipotle Powder

Nutrition

Prep: 10 min **Cook:** 4 h **Serves:** 3

Kcal per serve: 585 **Protein:** 56 g. (40%)
Fat: 40 g. (60%) **Carbs:** 0 g (0%)

Similar to Kahlua Pork... succulent, tender, and smoky, less all the hassle of having to dig up a deep roasting pit.

Tip: If you can, wrap the pork in a banana leaf for a real Hawaiian experience!

Preparation

1. Rub salt and liquid smoke all over the pork shoulder.
2. Set inside the pot, fat-side up.
3. Cook on slow cooker mode set high for 4 hours. Release pressure naturally.
4. Take the pork out of the pot and shred apart.
5. Take some of the cooking liquid in the pot and ladle onto the pulled pork meat.

Deonjang Pork Spare Ribs

NUTRITION

Prep: 10 min **Cook:** 25 min **Serves:** 4

High Fat Version
Kcal per serve: 448
Fat: 35 g. (70%)
Protein: 24 g. (23%)
Carbs: 9 g (7%)

Low Fat Version
Kcal per serve: 358
Fat: 25 g. (62%)
Protein: 24 g. (23%)
Carbs: 9 g (12%)

Bone-in cuts of pork and fermented soy bean paste blend in this rich, umami, Korean-inspired dish. Apples, soy sauce, sesame, and a few other choice aromatics only add further complexity.

Tip: Beef ribs or chicken thighs are good substitutes, too!

INGREDIENTS

Common Ingredients

- 1lb (450g) Pork Spare Ribs (lean and fat)
- 1/4 White Onion peeled and quartered
- 1 Scallions cut into 2" pieces
- 4 cloves Garlic crushed
- ½ Oz (15g.) Ginger thinly sliced
- 1/2 Apple grated
- 1/2 tbsp. Sesame Seeds
- 1 cup Pork Stock
- 1/2 tbsp. Soy Sauce
- 2 tbsp. Mirin / Dry wine
- 2 tbsp. Sweetener (zero calorie)
- 1 tbsp. Gochujang (or substitute)*

*Substitute: Chili peppers +Soy nsauce +Sugar

Low fat version ingredients
3 tbsp. Sesame Oil

High fat version ingredients
6 tbsp. Sesame Oil

PREPARATION

1. Combine stock, soy sauce, mirin, honey, sesame oil, gochujang (or substitute), apples, and sesame seeds in a blender. Process until smooth.

2. Arrange the pork ribs, onions, scallions, garlic, and ginger inside the pot.

3. Pour the blended sauce over the pork and cook on high pressure for 25 minutes. Quick release pressure.

Pork   17

Jamaican Jerk Pork Roast

NUTRITION

Prep: 10 min **Cook:** 20 min **Serves:** 4

Kcal per serve: 630 **Protein:** 48 g. (32%)
Fat: 45 g. (64%) **Carbs:** 6 g (4%)

Scrumptious juicy pork roast with a Jamaican jerk kick! With just four ingredients, this easy-to-make pork roast is a sure crowd pleaser!

Tip: Makes great leftovers!

INGREDIENTS

- 1 1/4 lb. pork shoulder (lean and fat)
- 4 tbsp. extra-virgin olive oil
- 1/4 cup Jamaican Jerk spice blend (cloves, ginger, and cinnamon with cayenne pepper)
- 1/2 cup beef stock

PREPARATION

1. Thoroughly rub pork roast with some of the oil and coat with spice blend.
2. Brown the meat in your instant pot under sauté mode and then add in beef broth.
3. Lock lid and cook on manual for 45 minutes and then release pressure naturally.
4. Remove roast and shred with fork. Drop over remaining oil. Serve.

Avocado & Bacon Stuffed Peppers

NUTRITION

Prep: 10 min   **Cook:** 5 min   **Serves:** 3

Kcal per serve: 420   **Protein:** 21 g. (21%)
Fat: 34 g. (71%)   **Carbs:** 9 g (8%)

INGREDIENTS

- 1/4 lb. (115g) sweet baby peppers
- 1/3 lb. (150g) chopped bacon
- 1/3 lb. (150g) ground beef
- 6 Oz (180g) ripe avocado
- 1 tbsp. hot sauce
- 2 tbsp. freshly squeezed lime juice
- ½ bunch cilantro, chopped
- Coarse sea salt

With just a few ingredients, these stuffed peppers are packed with creamy mixture topped with bacon –they are pressure baked to perfection.

Tip: Slice your bacon in half crosswise to create strips. Sauté bacon to your taste if you don't like it crispy.

PREPARATION

1. Add two cups of water to your instant pot and insert a trivet.
2. Cut the peppers in half, lengthwise, removing the seeds and membrane. Arrange them in a baking pan and lightly spray with cooking spray and place on the trivet. Lock lid and cook on manual for 5 minutes. Quick release pressure.
3. As the peppers are cooking, mash up the avocado in a bowl and combine with the hot sauce, lime juice, salt and the cilantro and sauté the bacon and ground beef in a skillet until they become crisp and browned.
4. Use a spoon to scoop the avocado mash into the peppers and top with bacon and beef bits. Enjoy!

Pork

Tuscan Herbed Pork Chops

Ingredients

Common Ingredients
- 1 cup (200 ml) Chicken Broth
- 1 tsp. (5 g.) Dried Thyme
- 1 tsp. (5 g.) Dried Oregano
- 1 tsp. (5 g.) Fresh Rosemary
- 1 tsp. (5 g.) Paprika
- ½ tsp. (2.5 g.) Black Pepper
- Salt, to taste

Low fat version ingredients
- 1.25 lbs. (500 g.) bone-in Pork Chops, Lean only
- ¼ cup (50 ml) Olive Oil
- ¾ cup (150 g.) Parmesan Cheese
- ½ cup (100 g.) Almond Flour
- 2 Eggs

High fat version ingredients
- 1 lb. (450 g.) bone-in Pork Chops, Lean only
- 9½ tbsp. (140 ml) Olive Oil
- 1 cup (200 g.) Parmesan Cheese
- ¼ cup (50 g.) Almond Flour
- 1 Egg

Nutrition

Prep: 5 min **Cook:** 25 min **Serves:** 4

High Fat Version
- Kcal per serve: 595
- Fat: 48 g. (71%)
- Protein: 35 g. (25%)
- Carbs: 6 g (4%)

Low Fat Version
- Kcal per serve: 485
- Fat: 32 g. (58%)
- Protein: 42 g. (37%)
- Carbs: 6 g (5%)

Parmesan crusted succulent pork chops flavoured with an assortment of Italian herbs and cooked to juicy perfection.

Tip: Chop up pork and toss on a salad for tomorrow's lunch!

Preparation

1. Wash the pork chops and pat dry. Mix the herbs and spices and rub onto the pork chops. Marinate for 1-2 hours
2. In the Instant Pot, place pork chops and broth inside and cook on high pressure for 5 minutes. Quick release pressure.
3. After releasing pressure, remove any remaining broth.
4. Heat olive oil in the cleaned Instant Pot.
5. Dredge chops in beaten egg and mixture of almond flour and parmesan. Sauté until a crispy coating is formed.

Minted Cream Soup

NUTRITION

Prep: 5 min   Cook: 30 min   Serves: 4

High Fat Version
Kcal per serve: 370
Fat: 29 g. (71%)
Protein: 18 g. (21%)
Carbs: 9 g (8%)

Low Fat Version
Kcal per serve: 310
Fat: 23 g. (65%)
Protein: 18 g. (24%)
Carbs: 9 g (11%)

Refreshing and light, with undertones of mint and juicy chunks of chicken, this cream soup is chilled thoroughly before serving. Easy and quick prep makes it ideal for serving in hot summers.

Tip: This recipe lends itself well for leftover chicken or even turkey. What's in the freezer you can use for this one?

INGREDIENTS

Common Ingredients
- 8 cups (1600 ml) Chicken Broth
- 1/8 cup (5 g.) Mint Leaves
- ½ cup (36 g.) Broccoli Florets
- ½ cup (34 g.) Kale
- 3/5 lb 250 g. Boneless Chicken Thigh
- 3 tbsp. (45 ml.) Lime Juice
- 1 cup (200 ml) Pureed Avocado
- Salt and pepper to taste

Low fat version ingredients
- ½ cup (100 ml) Light Sour Cream

High fat version ingredients
- ¾ cup (150 ml) Sour Cream

PREPARATION

1. In the Instant Pot, add all the ingredients except sour cream, salt and pepper. Cook for 10 minutes. Quick release pressure.
2. Take out chicken fillet and chop into small pieces.
3. Puree the rest of the contents. Add into instant Pot. Season with salt and pepper. Add chicken and heat until the soup simmers.
4. Chill thoroughly. Garnish with sour cream and serve.

Soup & Stews   21

Asparagus and Celery Soup

Ingredients

Common Ingredients
- 6 cups (1200 ml) Beef Broth
- ½ lb. (225 g.) Asparagus, cut into ½ inch pieces
- 1 cup (200 g) Celery, Chopped
- ½ tsp. (2.5 g.) Nutmeg, Grated
- ½ cup (100 g.) Cheddar Cheese, Shredded
- ½ cup (100 g.) Monterey Jack Cheese, Shredded
- 1 egg, beaten

Low fat version ingredients
- 3 tbsp. (45 g.) Salted Butter Light

High fat version ingredients
- 6 tbsp. (90 g.) Salted Butter

Nutrition

Prep: 5 min   **Cook:** 15 min   **Serves:** 3

High Fat Version
- Kcal per serve: 439
- Fat: 29 g. (78%)
- Protein: 19 g. (18%)
- Carbs: 5 g (4%)

Low Fat Version
- Kcal per serve: 315
- Fat: 24 g. (69%)
- Protein: 20 g. (25%)
- Carbs: 5 g (6%)

Low carb asparagus and celery soup made with flavourful beef broth with richness of cheese in every spoonful. Wholesome and hearty, serve for a cozy dinner on winter weekends.

Tip: Be sure to add a few leaves from the celery stalks for extra flavor as well as a pretty garnish when it's time to serve!

Preparation

1. In the Instant Pot, heat butter and sauté vegetables for 30 seconds
2. Add broth. Seal and cook low pressure for 6 minutes. Quick release pressure. Add egg into the soup slowly and keep mixing until ribbons begin to form.
3. Add shredded cheese and stir until melted. Add in seasonings and serve.

Chicken and Vegetable Soup

Ingredients

Common Ingredients

- 1 1/4 lb (560g.) ground chicken
- 1/2 medium red onion, diced
- 1/2 red bell pepper, diced
- 1/2 green bell pepper, diced
- 4 tsp. ground cumin
- 4 garlic cloves, minced
- 2 cups chopped spinach
- 4 cups water
- 1 tbsp. chopped chipotle chilis

Low fat version ingredients

- 2 tbsp. olive oil
- ½ Avocado

High fat version ingredients

- 4 tbsp. olive oil
- 1 Avocado

Nutrition

Prep: 10 min **Cook:** 18 min **Serves:** 4

High Fat Version
- Kcal per serve: 550
- Fat: 44 g. (71%)
- Protein: 29 g. (23%)
- Carbs: 9 g (6%)

Low Fat Version
- Kcal per serve: 445
- Fat: 33 g. (67%)
- Protein: 28 g. (27%)
- Carbs: 9 g (6%)

A comforting soup made with fat burning ingredients. Loaded with red onions, bell peppers, garlic and just the right amount of spices.

Tip: This soup keeps in the fridge up to a week.

Preparation

1. In a large skillet set over medium high heat, heat olive oil until hot but not smoky; sauté bell peppers and onion for about 8 minutes or until brown. Add ground chicken and cook until browned.

2. Stir in cumin and garlic for about 1 minute; transfer the mixture to your instant pot and then add water, chipotles and spinach and lock lid; cook on high pressure for 5 minutes and let pressure release naturally.

3. Transfer about 4 cups of the mixture to a blender and blend until very smooth.

4. Serve the soup into large soup bowls and top with diced avocado.

Soup & Stews

Spinach Chipotle Soup

NUTRITION

Prep: 20 min **Cook:** 35 min **Serves:** 3

High Fat Version
Kcal per serve: 550
Fat: 46 g. (74%)
Protein: 25 g. (19%)
Carbs: 9 g (7%)

Low Fat Version
Kcal per serve: 430
Fat: 32 g. (67%)
Protein: 25 g. (24%)
Carbs: 9 g (7%)

INGREDIENTS

Common Ingredients
- 1/2 lb. (225g.) ground beef
- 1 1/2 cups cauliflower florets, processed into cauliflower rice in a food processor
- 4 oz Spinach or 1/2 large leek, quartered then thinly sliced
- 3 cloves garlic crushed
- 3/4 cups coconut milk, full fat
- 1 cup vegetable stock
- 1/2 cracked dry chipotle pepper
- 1 bay leaf
- 1 tsp. herbs de Provence

Low fat version ingredients
- 2 tbsp. coconut oil

High fat version ingredients
- 5 tbsp. coconut oil

This herb infused creamy soup packs a nutritional punch to keep you full until your next meal.

Tip: Add a pinch of cayenne pepper for a hot and better taste. In case you do not have an immersion blender, transfer the content to your food processor and puree until smooth.

PREPARATION

1. Add the oil to your instant pot and set to sauté mode; cook the leek/spinach for 5 minutes until tender then stir in the garlic and cook until fragrant, for a minute or so, but don't let the garlic burn. Add beef and cook until browned and then add in the coconut milk, herbs, pepper, cauliflower rice and stock.

2. Give it a stir, lock lid and cook on high for 5 minutes. Let pressure come down on its own.

3. Remove the bay leaf and use an immersion blender to blend until smooth. Serve hot.

Spicy Beef Cauliflower Soup

NUTRITION

Prep: 10 min **Cook:** 14 min **Serves:** 4

Kcal per serve: 400 **Protein:** 32 g. (33%)
Fat: 26 g. (59%) **Carbs:** 8 g (8%)

Creamy and comforting, this recipe uses fresh vegetables and herbs from the garden together with convenient pantry ingredients to make an amazingly tasting soup.

Tip: Replace beef with chicken or turkey.

INGREDIENTS

- 1 lb (450g.) ground beef (80% lean meat)
- 2/3 cup diced carrot
- 1 cup diced red onion
- 1/8 teaspoon salt
- 4 tablespoons olive oil
- handful parsley
- 1 1/2 tablespoons curry powder
- 1/8 teaspoon pepper
- 2 cups diced cauliflower
- handful fresh thyme
- 2 2/3 cups water

PREPARATION

1. Heat oil in your instant pot and sauté red onion, cauliflower and carrots and cook for 4 minutes; stir in beef and cook until browned. Drain off excess grease. Stir in herbs and spices and water and lock lid.
2. Cook on manual for 10 minutes and then let pressure come down naturally.
3. Using an immersion blender, blend the pot content until very smooth.

Soup & Stews **25**

Crab & Winter Bamboo Shoot Egg Drop Soup

NUTRITION

Prep: 10 min **Cook:** 10 min **Serves:** 3

High Fat Version
- **Kcal** per serve: 445
- **Fat**: 34 g. (69%)
- **Protein**: 27 g. (25%)
- **Carbs**: 7 g (6%)

Low Fat Version
- **Kcal** per serve: 325
- **Fat**: 21 g. (58%)
- **Protein**: 27 g. (34%)
- **Carbs**: 7 g (8%)

Hot, comforting, and full of flavor. This Chinese-inspired egg drop soup is simply perfect for cold winter nights and rainy days.

Tip: Don't overbeat the eggs to keep the whites stringy. Add a shot of Sriracha for a burst of flavour!

INGREDIENTS

Common Ingredients
- 12 oz (340g.) Crab Meat
- 1 tsp. Red Chili Flakes
- 1 cup Bamboo Shoots/water chestnuts/Artichokes
- 1 tablespoon Soy Sauce
- ¼ cup Chopped Scallions/green onions
- 1 tablespoon Rice Vinegar
- 3 cups Chicken Broth
- 3 Large Eggs, beaten
- 1 tablespoon, Ginger Strips
- ½ teaspoon Ground White Pepper

Low fat version ingredients
- 1 tablespoon Sesame Oil
- 2 tablespoon Vegetable Oil

High fat version ingredients
- 2 tablespoon Sesame Oil
- 4 tablespoon Vegetable Oil

PREPARATION

1. Set pot to sauté mode.
2. Heat vegetable oil and sauté scallions, ginger, chili flakes until aromatic.
3. Add crab meat and bamboo shoots. Sauté briefly.
4. Add chicken broth, soy sauce, and vinegar. Bring to a simmer.
5. Gently stir in the beaten eggs. Allow to cook for about a minute.
6. Season with salt and pepper.
7. Drizzle on sesame oil before serving

Hearty Keto Beef Stew

Nutrition

Prep: 10 min **Cook:** 30 min **Serves:** 3

Kcal per serve: 530 **Protein:** 26 g. (20%)
Fat: 44 g. (75%) **Carbs:** 7 g (5%)

This healthy beef stew is the ultimate lunch hour comfort food especially during cold weather.

Tip: This stew can also be made in a slow cooker. Make sure the beef is lean and skin-free to make it low calorie.

Ingredients

- 1/2 lb.(225g.) bacon, diced
- 1/2 cup eggplant, cubed
- 1 clove garlic, chopped
- 1 tomato, chopped
- 1/2 lb. beef (chuck eye roast, boneless lean only), cubed
- 1/2 cup onion, chopped
- 2 cups water
- 1/2 tbsp. spice mix (cumin, turmeric, cinnamon, paprika, and red pepper)
- 1/2 cup shredded cabbage
- 2 tbsp. coconut oil
- 1 carrot, thinly sliced

Preparation

1. Set your instant pot on sauté mode and add coconut oil; sauté red onion, garlic and bacon until bacon is browned.
2. Add beef and cook until beef is browned and then add the remaining ingredients and lock lid and cook on manual for 30 minutes.
3. Let pressure come down on its own.

Soup & Stews

Spicy Masala Lamb Chops

Ingredients

Common Ingredients
- ½ cup (100 ml) Beef Broth
- 4 tbsp. (60 g.) Tandoori Masala
- 2 tbsp. (30 ml) Lemon Juice
- 1 tbsp. (15 g.) Minced Garlic
- 1 tsp. (5 g) Cayenne Pepper
- 2-3 Cinnamon Sticks
- Salt and black pepper to taste

Low fat version ingredients
- 2 lbs (900 g.) Lamb Chops, Bone in, Lean
- 1 cup (200 ml) Low Fat Plain Yogurt
- 4 tbsp. (60 g.) Tandoori Masala
- 5 tsb canola oil

High fat version ingredients
- 1 ½ lbs (680 g.) Lamb Chops, Bone in, Trimmed to ¼ fat
- ¾ cup (150 ml) Low Fat Plain Yogurt
- 1/3 cup (85 g.) Light Whipping Cream

Nutrition

Prep: 10 min **Cook:** 15 min **Serves:** 4

High Fat Version
- Kcal per serve: 642
- Fat: 54 g. (80%)
- Protein: 31 g. (%)
- Carbs: 8 g (4%)

Low Fat Version
- Kcal per serve: 463
- Fat: 27 g. (59%)
- Protein: 49 g. (37%)
- Carbs: 6 g (4%)

Aromatic lamb chops spiced up with tandoori flavours, then cooked in its own juices make for a delicious meal. Perfect for serving on a game night with friends.

Preparation

1. Mix the yogurt, cream, lemon juice, salt and spices in a large bowl.
2. Add the lamb chops to the yogurt mixture and coat well.
3. Leave the lamb chops to marinate overnight in the refrigerator.
4. Once it has finished marinating, add all the ingredients and lock lid into place. Then set the steam release handle to 'Sealing'. Select Manual and cook at high pressure for 15 minutes.
5. After the times is up, let pressure be released naturally for 10 minutes, and after flip the steam release handle to "Venting" mode, letting the rest of steam go before trying to open the lid.

Port Wine Lamb Shanks

NUTRITION

Prep: 15 min   **Cook:** 40 min   **Serves:** 3

Kcal per serve: 495   **Protein:** 37 g. (30%)
Fat: 34 g. (62%)   **Carbs:** 10 g (8%)

Lamb shanks are a fantastic and versatile cut of meat.

Tip: Give the sauce extra richness and a lovely glossy sheen by adding butter. After stirring in the parsley (step 6) add a tablespoon or two of cold butter to the sauce. Vigorously whisk in the butter until dissolved and it has been incorporated into the sauce.

INGREDIENTS

- 1 lb. lamb shanks
- 1 1/2 cups ruby Port wine
- 1 tsp. dried thyme
- sea salt to taste
- 5 tbsp olive oil
- 1 cup chicken or veal stock
- 1 tsp. dried rosemary
- 3 tbsp. unsalted butter
- 1/2 large red onion, diced
- 1 tbsp. tomato paste
- 3 tsp. dried parsley
- 3 tsp. Sherry vinegar
- 5 cloves garlic, peeled and halved
- 1/2 can (7oz, 210g.) chopped tomatoes
- 1 tsp. freshly ground black pepper, or to taste

PREPARATION

1. Set the Instant Pot to Sauté (More/High) and add the oil. When hot brown the lamb shanks all over, one at a time. Set aside in a bowl to capture any juices.

2. Set to Sauté (Less) and add the onion and garlic and cook until soft. Set to Off.

3. Add the lamb juices from the bowl, Port wine, stock, tomato paste, chopped tomatoes, herbs, pepper and salt and stir to combine. Add the lamb shanks and spoon over the liquid to coat them well.

4. Place on the lid and set to Manual (More/High) for 30 minutes. When done switch off and allow the pressure to release naturally. Remove the lamb shanks to a warmed serving dish and cover to keep warm.

5. Set to Sauté (More). Add the butter and vigorously whisk in until incorporated. Stir in vinegar to taste and pour the sauce over the lamb shanks.

6. whisk in the butter until dissolved and it has been incorporated into the sauce.

Lamb

Grilled Lamb & Veggies Bowl

Ingredients

Common Ingredients

- 1 cup dried mushrooms
- 1 cup water
- 2 cloves garlic, minced
- 12 ounces grilled lamb, diced
- 1 cup baby arugula
- 1/2 cup sweet potato slices
- 1/2 cup red pepper, chopped
- 1/2 cup scallions, chopped
- 2 tsp. fresh cilantro leaves
- 2 tbsp. tomato sauce

Low fat version ingredients

- 2 tbsp. olive oil

High fat version ingredients

- 4 tbsp. olive oil

Nutrition

Prep: 10 min **Cook:** 20 min **Serves:** 3

High Fat Version
- **Kcal** per serve: 510
- **Fat**: 40 g. (70%)
- **Protein**: 30 g. (24%)
- **Carbs**: 7 g (5%)

Low Fat Version
- **Kcal** per serve: 430
- **Fat**: 31 g. (70%)
- **Protein**: 30 g. (24%)
- **Carbs**: 7 g (5%)

This healthy instant pot cooked grilled lamb dish will help you forget fast foods and achieve your weight loss goals.

Tip: This is a great entrée that reheats well for lunch at the desk!

Preparation

1. Combine mushrooms, water and garlic in your instant pot. Cook on high for 5 minutes and then release the pressure naturally.

2. Meanwhile, grill lamb to medium rare for about 15 minutes. Grill scallions, red pepper, and sweet potatoes along with the lamb until tender.

3. Place cooked mushrooms in a bowl; top with grilled lamb, scallions, veggies, peppers, cilantro, and microgreens.

4. In a bowl, whisk oil, tomato sauce, salt, and pepper; drizzle over steak mixture and serve drizzled with lime juice.

Lamb Leg with Gravy

INGREDIENTS

Common Ingredients

- 1 lb (450 g.) boneless leg of lamb
- 1 tsp. garlic powder
- 1 tbsp. onion powder
- 1 tsp. dried thyme
- 1/2 cup wine vinegar
- 1 1/2 cups water
- 1 tsp seasoned salt
- 1 tsp. cayenne/paprika/red chilli
- A pinch of pepper
- 2 tbsp. chopped herbs (parsley, basil, rosemary and oregano)

For the gravy (common)

- 2 tbsp. almond flour
- 1 tbsp. minced shallot
- 1 tbsp. minced garlic
- salt and pepper
- 1/2 tsp water

Low fat version ingredients

- 2 tbsp. Olive Oil

For the gravy (low fat)

- 2 tbsp. melted coconut oil

High fat version ingredients

- 4 tbsp. Olive Oil

For the gravy (high fat)

- 4 tbsp. melted coconut oil

NUTRITION

Prep: 15 min   **Cook:** 2 h   **Serves:** 3

High Fat Version
- Kcal per serve: 570
- Fat: 45 g. (71%)
- Protein: 32 g. (24%)
- Carbs:- 10 g (5%)

Low Fat Version
- Kcal per serve: 415
- Fat: 27 g. (59%)
- Protein: 32 g. (34%)
- Carbs: 10 g (7%)

Another easier than it sounds recipe that is sure to please the family.

Tip: Double up on the protein portion without making more sauce!

PREPARATION

1. Season the lamb with garlic powder, onion powder, thyme, salt and pepper.
2. Add half of olive oil to your instant pot and set it on sauté mode; add lamb and cook for about 5 minutes per side or until browned and then transfer to a plate.
3. Add vinegar to the pot and simmer for a minute, while scraping bits of lamb stuck in the pot; turn off the pot and stir in water and then add in the lamb; lock lid and cook on high for 90 minutes and then let pressure come down naturally. Meanwhile preheat your oven at 400 °F.
4. Transfer the cooked lamb to a baking dish and drizzle with the remaining oil; top with herb mix and bake in the oven for about 15 minutes or until browned.
5. Make gravy: pour the cooking liquid to a bowl and skim off fat; add coconut oil to the instant pot and turn on sauté mode; stir in shallots, garlic and flour until well combined and then gradually whisk in two cups of cooking liquid. Stir for about 5 minutes or until gravy is thick and then stir in salt and pepper. Serve lamb topped with gravy and fresh parsley. Enjoy!

Lamb

Lamb Ribs

Ingredients

Common Ingredients
- 1 lb. (450 g.) Lamb Ribs, Lean, Bone in
- 1½ cup (300 ml) Beef Broth
- 1/3 cup (80 ml) Light Cream
- ½ cup (100 ml) Shredded Low Fat Cheddar Cheese
- 2 tbsp. (30 ml) Lime Juice
- 1 tsp. (5 g.) Paprika
- 1 tsp. (5 g.) Black Pepper
- Salt, to taste

Low fat version ingredients
- 1/4 cup (50 ml) Olive Oil

High fat version ingredients
- 1/3 cup (50 ml) Olive Oil

Nutrition

Prep: 5 min **Cook:** 15 min **Serves:** 4

High Fat Version
- Kcal per serve: 590
- Fat: 48 g. (72%)
- Protein: 37 g. (27%)
- Carbs: 3 g (2%)

Low Fat Version
- Kcal per serve: 540
- Fat: 42 g. (69%)
- Protein: 37 g. (29%)
- Carbs: 3 g (2%)

A hearty dinner for a special occasion or a relaxing weekend.

Tip: Serve with marinated cucumbers and kalamata olives for a tangy complement to the creamy cheese sauce!

Preparation

1. Mix together salt, black pepper, paprika, lime juice and rub onto the lamb ribs.
2. Heat oil in the Instant Pot and sautéed the ribs until they change colour.
3. Add beef broth and cook on high pressure for 8 minutes. Release pressure naturally.
4. Remove ribs. Add cream and cheese to the Instant Pot. Mix with the leftover broth until cheese is melted.
5. Spoon over ribs and serve.

Luscious Lamb Skewers

INGREDIENTS

Common Ingredients
- 2 cups (400 ml) Beef Broth
- 1 cup (200 ml) Non-Alcoholic Wine
- 2 tbsp. (30 ml) Lemon Juice
- ½ cup (13 g.) Fresh Parsley
- 2 Garlic Cloves, Minced
- Few sprigs of rosemary and thyme
- ½ cup (80 g.) Finely Chopped Onion
- Pepper and salt to taste

Low fat version ingredients
- 2 lbs (900 g.) Boneless Lamb, Lean, cut into cubes

High fat version ingredients
- 2 lbs (900 g.) Boneless Lamb, Lean and Fat, cut into cubes with ¼' Fat

NUTRITION

Prep: 10 min **Cook:** 15 min **Serves:** 4

High Fat Version
- **Kcal** per serve: 550
- **Fat:** 46 g. (75%)
- **Protein:** 30 g. (23%)
- **Carbs:** 4 g (2%)

Low Fat Version
- **Kcal** per serve: 320
- **Fat:** 12 g. (33%)
- **Protein:** 49 g. (63%)
- **Carbs:** 4 g (5%)

Succulent pieces of lamb infused with a fragrant broth and finished off by smothering in a rich wine sauce. Satisfy your kebob cravings by preparing these aromatic skewers packing a flavorful punch.

Tip: Use the freshest cuts of meat you can find. If you can't find lamb, chicken will do!

PREPARATION

1. Rub salt and pepper on the lamb cubes and thread onto skewers.
2. In the Instant Pot, heat butter oil and sauté until the lamb cubes begin to change colour.
3. Remove skewers and pour broth, rosemary and thyme, garlic and parsley in the Pot.
4. Place lamb skewers on the trivet and cook on high pressure for 10 minutes. Release Pressure naturally.
5. Remove skewers and trivet.
6. Add wine to the pot and cook sauce for 10 minutes or until thickened. Pour over skewers and serve.

Lamb

Balsamic & Rosemary Roast Beef

NUTRITION

Prep: 15 min **Cook:** 4 1/2 h **Serves:** 3

Kcal per serve: 570 Protein: 39 g. (9%)
Fat: 42 g. (66%) Carbs: 8 g (5%)

Spicy balsamic and earthy rosemary flavours will make this delicious beef roast an absolute favorite. Slice into strips and serve over a bed of lettuce for a protein-packed salad!

INGREDIENTS

- 1 lb. (450 g.) beef rump roast
- 3 tbsp. olive, canola or vegetable oil
- 1/2 large red onion, chopped
- 2 cloves garlic, crushed
- 2 tbsp. coarse ground black pepper, to taste
- 2 stalks fresh rosemary
- 2 bay leaves/Thyme/Juniper Berries
- 1 tbsp. balsamic vinegar
- 1 tsp. sherry vinegar
- 1 tbsp. dark soy sauce
- ½ cup beef or veal stock
- 1 tbsp. Dijon mustard
- 1 tbsp. muscovado or dark brown sugar
- 1/2 small bunch parsley, chopped

PREPARATION

1. Set the Instant Pot to Sauté (More/High) and add the oil. When hot add the beef roast and brown on all sides. Set aside the beef in a bowl.

2. Select Sauté (Less), add the onions and garlic and cook until soft. Add the black pepper, rosemary and bay leaves. Switch the Instant Pot off.

3. Add the remaining ingredients, including the juices from the beef, and stir to combine.

4. Set the Instant Pot to Slow (Normal) for 4 hours. Add the roast and pour liquid mixture over the top of the roast and secure the lid, ensuring the vent switch is set to open. Release pressure naturally.

5. When done remove the beef to a warm serving dish. Remove the rosemary stalks. Taste the sauce and add salt if desired.

6. Set the Instant Pot to Sauté (More) and stir in the parsley. Cook for a few minutes to thicken the sauce if necessary.

Oatmeal Beef Meatballs

NUTRITION

Prep: 10 min **Cook:** 20 min **Serves:** 4

High Fat Version
Kcal per serve: 445
Fat: 39 g. (78%)
Protein: 18 g. (16%)
Carbs: 7 g (5%)

Low Fat Version
Kcal per serve: 330
Fat: 20 g. (55%)
Protein: 30 g. (38%)
Carbs: 7 g (7%)

Tip: Make the meatballs with other types of ground meat, such as turkey or chicken. White meat is waterier, so consider reducing the amount of liquid you use.

INGREDIENTS

Common Ingredients
- 1/2 cup of rolled oats
- 2 tablespoons onion flakes
- ½ cup of milk
- 1 egg
- 2 tablespoons coconut oil
- a pinch of salt and pepper to taste

Non-Keto Sauce
- Brown sugar to taste
- 3 oz tomato sauce
- 4 baby tomatoes, crushed
- Smoke BBQ sauce to taste
- Oz Beef broth
- Salt & Pepper to taste

Low fat version ingredients
14.0 oz (400 g.) ground beef (90% lean / 10% fat)

High fat version ingredients
14.0 oz (400 g.) ground beef (70% lean / 30% fat)

PREPARATION

1. In a food processor, blend the rolled oats, onion flakes, salt and pepper. Process until the oat resembles a coarse meal. Set aside.

2. In a bowl, whisk the milk and the egg. Break up the ground beef with your fingers. Add the ground beef to the egg and milk mixture. Mix well. Then, add the oatmeal. Add more milk if the mixture is too dry. Form the beef mixture into 1-inch balls or approximately the size of a golf ball.

3. Make the sauce. In a bowl, whisk the brown sugar, tomato sauce, crushed tomatoes, hickory smoke barbecue sauce, beef broth, salt, & pepper.

4. In the Instant Pot set to sauté, heat 2 tablespoons of coconut oil. You may us olive oil, but personally, I prefer coconut oil because our body processes and turns coconut oil into energy faster than other vegetable oil.

5. Once the oil is hot, sear the meatballs, turning them occasionally to prevent burning, until the outer part forms golden brown crusts.

6. Add the sauce into the pot. Close the lid and cook on low pressure for 30 minutes.

7. Let the pressure out via quick release.

8. Serve the meatball on top of a mashed potato, baked potato, boiled pasta or steamed vegetables.

Beef

Scrumptious Italian Beef with Avocado

Ingredients

Common Ingredients
- 2 cloves garlic
- 1 tsp. marjoram/Thyme
- 1 tsp. basil
- 1 tsp. oregano
- 1/3 cup coconut cream
- 1/2 tsp. ground ginger
- 3 tbsp. olive oil
- 1 tsp. onion powder
- 1 tsp. garlic powder
- 1 tsp. salt
- 1/4 cup apple cider vinegar
- 6 oz. (180g.) raw avocado, sliced
- 1 cup water

Low fat version ingredients
- 1 lb. (450 g.) grass-fed chuck roast (lean only)

High fat version ingredients
- 3/4 lb. (330g.) grass-fed chuck roast lean and fat (85% lean 15% fat)

Nutrition

Prep: 10 min   **Cook:** 30 min   **Serves:** 3

High Fat Version
- Kcal per serve: 595
- Fat: 52 g. (78%)
- Protein: 23 g. (15%)
- Carbs: 9 g (6%)

Low Fat Version
- Kcal per serve: 500
- Fat: 35 g. (62%)
- Protein: 37 g. (30%)
- Carbs: 9 g (7%)

When it comes to following a weight loss regimen, eating healthy is essential to keep away the cravings.

Tip: Choose cuts of meat with some marbling. Fat means flavor and totally okay on Keto!

Preparation

1. Cut slits in the roast with a sharp knife and then stuff with garlic cloves.

2. Heat oil in the instant pot under sauté mode. In a bowl, whisk together marjoram, basil, oregano, ground ginger, onion powder, garlic powder, and salt until well blended; rub the seasoning all over the roast and place it in your instant pot; cook until beef is browned on both sides.

3. Add vinegar and water and lock lid; cook on high for 90 minutes. Release pressure naturally and then shred meat with a fork; stir in coconut cream.

4. Serve along with cooking juices topped with avocado.

Ground Beef Skewers

NUTRITION

Prep: 20 min **Cook:** 15 min **Serves:** 4

High Fat Version
Kcal per serve: 600
Fat: 48 g. (72%)
Protein: 39 g. (26%)
Carbs: 4 g (2%)

Low Fat Version
Kcal per serve: 562
Fat: 38 g. (61%)
Protein: 51 g. (37%)
Carbs: 4 g (3%)

Inspired from Persian cuisine, delectable ground beef skewers packed full of fiery spice and cooked to perfection. These appetizing skewers are perfect for taking to a potluck or enjoying as an outstanding midweek dinner.

Tip: Soak skewers in water 30 minutes before using to make sure they don't burn!

INGREDIENTS

Common Ingredients
- ¼ cup (40 g.) Chopped Onion
- ¼ cup (15 g.) Cilantro (Finely Chopped)
- 1 Egg
- 3 tbsp. (45 ml) Lemon Juice
- 1-2 Chilli Pepper (Finely Chopped)
- 1 tsp. (5 g.) Black Pepper
- 1 tsp. (5 g.) Chilli Powder
- ¾ tsp. (3.5 g.) Salt

Low fat version ingredients
- 2 lbs. (900 g.) Ground Beef (95% Lean)
- ½ cup (100 g.) Ghee

High fat version ingredients
- 1 1/2 lbs (680 g.) Ground Beef (95% Lean)
- ¾ cup (150 g.) Ghee

PREPARATION

1. In a large bowl, thoroughly combine all the ingredients to form a uniform mixture except ghee.
2. Take a small ball of the mixture and form a cylindrical shape about 3 inches long around the skewer. Repeat until all the beef mixture is used up.
3. Brush the skewers with ghee.
4. Place lamb skewers on the trivet and cook on high pressure for 10 minutes.
5. Release Pressure naturally. Remove skewers and trivet.

Beef

Sweet Peppercorn Salmon

NUTRITION

Prep: 5 min **Cook:** 15 min **Serves:** 4

High Fat Version	Low Fat Version
Kcal per serve: 525	**Kcal** per serve: 395
Fat: 42 g. (71%)	**Fat**: 28 g. (62%)
Protein: 33 g. (26%)	**Protein**: 32 g. (35%)
Carbs: 4 g (3%)	**Carbs**: 4 g (4%)

Scrumptious fillets of Salmon seasoned with freshly crushed peppercorn, paired with a sweet and sour sauce bring about an explosion of flavors. Spice up your midweek meals with this tangy salmon dish.

Tip: Look for salmon that is succulent and free of blemishes. Ideally, look for bright pink or orange flesh.

INGREDIENTS

Common Ingredients
- 4 (600 g.) Salmon Fillets
- 2 tbsp. (8 g.) Parsley
- 1 tbsp. (15 ml) Lemon Juice
- 2 tbsp. (30 ml) Peanut Sauce
- 1 tbsp. (15 ml) Apple Cider Vinegar
- 1 tsp. (5 g.) Black Pepper, coarsely ground
- ½ tsp. (2.5 g.) Minced Ginger
- Salt, to taste
- 1 pinch Stevia Concentrate (optional)

Low fat version ingredients
- ½ cup (100 ml) Heavy Cream
- 3 tbsp. (45 g.) Butter

High fat version ingredients
- ¾ cup (150 ml) Heavy Cream
- 6 tbsp. (90 g.) Butter

PREPARATION

1. Select the Sauté option on the Instant Pot and add butter, ginger, stevia, lemon juice, vinegar and peanut sauce. Cook for about a minute.

2. Rub the salmon fillets with salt and pepper and place inside the Instant Pot. Spoon sauce over the fillets. Add ¼ cup water and cook on low pressure for 1 minute.

3. Release pressure manually. Flip with care and sauté salmon until cooked to your liking. Take out salmon from the pot and let the sauce simmer for an additional 3 to 4 minutes. Add heavy cream and stir until well combined.

4. Drizzle sauce over the fillets and garnish with parsley.

Seafood Medley Stew

Ingredients

Common Ingredients

- 2 cups (400 ml) Chicken Broth
- ½ lb. (225 g.) Shrimp
- ½ lb. (225 g.) Mussels
- ½ cup (100 ml) Coconut Cream
- 100 g. Fish (Salmon or Halibut)
- 1-2 Bay Leaves
- 2 tbsp. (30 ml) Lemon Juice
- 1 tbsp. (15 g.) Ginger, Minced
- 2 cloves Garlic, Crushed
- ½ tsp. (2.5 g.) Black Pepper
- 1 Dried Whole Star Anise

Low fat version ingredients

- ¾ cup (150 ml) Light Cream
- 2 tbsp. (30 ml) Coconut Oil

High fat version ingredients

- 1 cup (200 ml) Light Cream
- 3 tbsp. (45 ml) Coconut Oil

Nutrition

Prep: 5 min **Cook:** 20 min **Serves:** 3

High Fat Version
- Kcal per serve: 535
- Fat: 44 g. (73%)
- Protein: 27 g. (21%)
- Carbs: 8 g (6%)

Low Fat Version
- Kcal per serve: 460
- Fat: 36 g. (69%)
- Protein: 26 g. (24%)
- Carbs: 8 g (7%)

Zesty stew with a combination of the best seafood flavors all wrapped in one. With its hassle-free preparation, this coconut flavoured stew is perfect for when you're pressed for time. Ideal for serving on a cold winter weeknight.

Tip: Spices can be expensive! Be sure you are storing them in a cool space and out of direct light or heat sources to ensure maximum flavor and freshness!.

Preparation

1. In the Instant Pot, sauté the bay leaves and star anise in coconut oil for about 30 seconds.
2. Add ginger and garlic. Continue to sauté.
3. Add broth. Rub lemon juice, salt and pepper on fish fillets and place in the Pot. Add shrimp and mussels as well.
4. Cook for 10 minutes. Release pressure naturally.
5. Add the two creams and allow to simmer.
6. Remove bay leaves and star anise before serving.

Fish & Seafood

Lemon Kalamata Olive Salmon

INGREDIENTS

Common Ingredients

- 4 x 5oz (140g) salmon filets
- ¼ tsp. black pepper
- 1 tsp. herbes de Provence (savoury, oregano, thyme and fennel seeds)
- 1 tsp. sea salt
- 1 cup fish broth
- 2 tbsp. fresh lemon juice
- ½ cup red onion, sliced
- 1 can pitted kalamata olives/ black olives/capers
- ½ lemon, thinly sliced
- ½ tsp. cumin

Low fat version ingredients

- ¼ cup olive oil

High fat version ingredients

- ½ cup olive oil

NUTRITION

Prep: 10 min   **Cook:** 20 min   **Serves:** 3

High Fat Version
- Kcal per serve: 440
- Fat: 34 g. (68%)
- Protein: 30 g. (3%)
- Carbs: 3 g (2%)

Low Fat Version
- Kcal per serve: 320
- Fat: 20 g. (56%)
- Protein: 31 g. (41%)
- Carbs: 4 g (3%)

Spiced-infused olive oil and all citrusy goodness makes this dish amazing!

Tip: Substitute Herbes de Provence with fresh herbs– a mix of fresh basil, parsley, and oregano– surely set to become your all-time favourite once you try it!

PREPARATION

1. Generously season salmon filets with cumin, pepper and salt; set your instant pot on sauté mode and heat the olive oil; add fish and brown both sides.

2. Stir the remaining ingredients into the pot and bring to a simmer; lock lid. Set your pot on manual high for 10 minutes; when done, quick release pressure and then serve.

Creamy Chile Shrimp

NUTRITION

Prep: 5 min **Cook:** 20 min **Serves:** 3

High Fat Version
Kcal per serve: 555
Fat: 45 g. (72%)
Protein: 33 g. (23%)
Carbs: 7 g (5%)

Low Fat Version
Kcal per serve: 395
Fat: 27 g. (60%)
Protein: 33 g. (33%)
Carbs: 7 g (7%)

Shrimp is easy to cook and is packed with nutrients. This recipe is just a little bit spicy, but you can always add or decrease the chiles to suit your palate!

Tip: When chilled, this recipe is great on a salad!

INGREDIENTS

Common Ingredients

- 1 lb. (450 g.) Shrimp
- ½ cup (50 g.) Bell Pepper, cut into thin strips
- ½ cup (45 g.) White Cabbage
- ½ cup (100 ml) Chicken Stock
- ½ cup (100 ml) Heavy Cream
- 1 tbsp. (15 g.) Garlic, minced
- 1 Chile Pepper, cut into thin strips
- 1 tbsp. (15 g.) Ginger, cut into thin long strips
- ½ tsp. (2.5 g.) Cayenne Powder
- ½ tsp. (2.5 g.) Black Pepper
- ½ tsp. (2.5 ml) Hot Sauce
- ½ tsp. (2.5 ml) Lime Juice

Low fat version ingredients

- ¼ cup (50 ml) Canola Oil

High fat version ingredients

- ½ cup (100 ml) Canola Oil

PREPARATION

1. Deseed and cut the green chile into thin strips lengthwise.

2. In the Instant Pot, sauté the bell pepper, cabbage and green chilli with half oil for 3-4 minutes. Remove and keep warm by covering with foil.

3. Sautee ginger and garlic in the Instant Pot with the rest of the oil and add shrimp. Turn off sauté function. Add the spices, hot sauce and Lime Juice.

4. Add chicken stock and cook on high pressure for 4 minutes. Quick pressure release and add the sautéed vegetables and mix well.

5. Add cream and sauté until the sauce thickens slightly. Serve.

Fish & Seafood

Baked Cod

INGREDIENTS

Common Ingredients

- 2 oz (60g) cherry tomatoes
- Pinch of salt & pepper
- 1 tbsp. chili seasoning mix
- 4 oz (120g.) Raw Avocado

Low fat version ingredients	High fat version ingredients
1lb. (450 g.) Atlantic cod filet, sliced into pieces	¾ lb. (330 g.) Atlantic cod filet, sliced into pieces
2 tbsp. melted coconut oil	4 tbsp. melted coconut oil
1 tbsp Olive oil	2 tbsp Olive oil

NUTRITION

Prep: 2 min   **Cook:** 5 min   **Serves:** 3

High Fat Version	Low Fat Version
Kcal per serve: 480	Kcal per serve: 395
Fat: 39 g. (74%)	Fat: 28 g. (62%)
Protein: 23 g. (19%)	Protein: 29 g. (30%)
Carbs: 9 g (7%)	Carbs: 9 g (9%)

Cod is loaded with omega-2 fatty acids and has a mild flavour. Enjoy every single bite of this simple but nutritious lunch.

Tip: You can use foil instead of a baking dish —lay the foil directly on the trivet and lay tomatoes on top; top with fish and season; drizzle with oil and lock lid.

PREPARATION

1. Add tomatoes in an oven-safe dish. Lay fish pieces over the tomatoes; season with seasoning, salt and pepper and drizzle with melted coconut oil.

2. Add a cup of water in your instant pot and add a trivet.

3. Place the dish in the pot and lock lid; cook on manual for 5 minutes and then let pressure come down on its own. Serve along with peeled avocado on the side and season with olive oil.

Vegetable Hash

Ingredients

Common Ingredients
- 1 cups cauliflower, chopped
- 1/2 cup chopped dark-leaf kale
- 1/2 cup chopped spinach
- 2 cloves garlic
- 1 tsp. mustard
- 1 tbsp. lemon juice
- ½ tsp. sea salt
- ½ tsp. pepper

Low fat version ingredients
- 6 egg whites
- 2 tsp coconut oil or ghee

High fat version ingredients
- 6 whole eggs
- 3 tsp coconut oil or ghee

Nutrition

Prep: 10 min   Cook: 15 min   Serves: 3

High Fat Version
Kcal per serve: 430
Fat: 35 g. (72%)
Protein: 22 g. (21%)
Carbs: 8 g (7%)

Low Fat Version
Kcal per serve: 210
Fat: 14 g. (60%)
Protein: 14 g. (27%)
Carbs: 8 g (14%)

A mash made with healthy ingredients such as cauliflower, dark-green kale and spinach to help you burn excess fat. So tasty that it will become your favourite go-to healthy vegetarian meal.

Tip: Always wash/rinse your fresh produce to avoid consuming pesticides.

Preparation

1. Set your instant pot on sauté mode and melt coconut oil or ghee; add garlic and cook until fragrant and then stir in chopped cauliflower.
2. Cook for about 5 minutes and then stir in the remaining ingredients, except eggs; cook for about 2 minutes.
3. Stir in the eggs and lock lid, cook on high for 2 minutes and then quick release pressure.
4. Enjoy!

Vegetarian   43

Egg Frittata

INGREDIENTS

Common Ingredients

- 5 Whole Eggs
- 1 cup (30 g.) Spinach
- ½ cup (20 g.) Mushrooms
- ¾ tsp. Mixed Herbs
- ¼ cup (50 g.) Shredded Cheddar Cheese
- Salt and pepper, to taste

Low fat version ingredients

- ¾ cup (150 ml) Low Fat Half and Half (half milk half cream)
- 2 tbsp. (30 g.) Butter

High fat version ingredients

- ¾ cup (150 ml) Half and Half (half milk half cream)
- 2 tbsp. (30 g.) Butter

NUTRITION

Prep: 10 min   **Cook:** 15 min   **Serves:** 3

High Fat Version	Low Fat Version
Kcal per serve: 300	**Kcal** per serve: 255
Fat: 25 g. (74%)	**Fat**: 19 g. (68%)
Protein: 14 g. (20%)	**Protein**: 14 g. (23%)
Carbs: 4 g (6%)	**Carbs**: 6 g (9%)

Whether you're looking for a wholesome breakfast, or a hasty but enjoyable dinner, this egg frittata will become your go-to recipe.

Tip: Always select eggs that are fresh and free from cracks or unpleasant odors.

PREPARATION

1. Dice mushrooms and chop spinach leaves finely.
2. Melt butter and sauté spinach and mushrooms in the Instant Pot.
3. Whisk the eggs and add milk, cream, cheese, herbs and the sautéed vegetables. Add salt and pepper according to your liking and mix well.
4. Grease a 6-inch baking pan and pour the mixture in it.
5. In the Instant Pot, add about 2 cups of water and place the pan on the trivet.
6. Cook for 10 minutes, then release pressure naturally.

Scrambled Tofu

NUTRITION

Prep: 15 min   Cook: 15 min   Serves: 2

High Fat Version	Low Fat Version
Kcal per serve: 430	**Kcal** per serve: 300
Fat: 34 g. (73%)	**Fat**: 20 g. (61%)
Protein: 24 g. (20%)	**Protein**: 24 g. (29%)
Carbs: 7 g (7%)	**Carbs**: 7 g (10%)

INGREDIENTS

Common Ingredients

- 2 cups chopped broccoli floret
- 1 lb. extra firm tofu
- 2 cloves garlic, crushed

Spice mix (common)

- ½ tsp sweet paprika
- pinch cardamom powder
- ½ tsp cumin
- ½ tsp curry powder
- ¼ tsp dried thyme
- ½ tsp sea salt or to taste
- Pinch of cinnamon powder

Low fat version ingredients

- 1 tbsp. olive oil

High fat version ingredients

- 2 tbsp. olive oil

PREPARATION

1. Sauté the garlic and broccoli in olive oil on sauté mode in your instant pot for about 2 minutes, stirring constantly so the garlic doesn't burn.

2. Add the tofu and cook until it browns evenly, keep turning with a metallic spatula so the tofu doesn't stick. This will ensure that the tofu attains a delicious crunch instead of the crust being left on the pan. Lock lid and cook on high pressure for 2 minutes; release pressure naturally.

3. As the tofu is cooking, combine the spice mix in a small bowl and add 2 tablespoons of water and stir well. Add the spice mix to the tofu scramble, stirring well. Cover with lid and press sauté mode to cook for about 5 minutes and turn off the heat. Serve immediately. Enjoy!

Vegetarian

Coconut Cabbage

Nutrition

Prep: 10 min   **Cook:** 7 min   **Serves:** 2

High Fat Version
- **Kcal** per serve: 400
- **Fat:** 34 g. (75%)
- **Protein:** 14 g. (15%)
- **Carbs:** 10 g (10%)

Low Fat Version
- **Kcal** per serve: 265
- **Fat:** 18 g. (61%)
- **Protein:** 15 g. (24%)
- **Carbs:** 10 g (10%)

Here's a healthy twist on a cabbage dish.

Tip: Mash up avocado and combine it with finely chopped coriander, chili and about a tablespoon of lime juice. Add this to your hot cabbage for a creamy and healthy meal.

Ingredients

Common Ingredients
- 2 tablespoons lemon juice
- 1/3 medium carrot, sliced
- 1/2 oz (15 g.) yellow onion, sliced
- ½ cup cabbage, shredded
- 1 teaspoon turmeric powder
- 1 oz. dry coconut
- 1/2 tablespoon mild curry powder
- 1 teaspoon mustard powder
- 1 large cloves of garlic, diced
- 1 ½ teaspoons salt
- 1/3 cup water

Low fat version ingredients
- 1.5 tablespoon coconut oil
- 2 large whole eggs
- 4 large egg whites

High fat version ingredients
- 3 tablespoon olive oil
- 3 large whole eggs
- 3 large egg yolks

Preparation

1. Turn your instant pot on sauté mode and add oil; stir in onion and salt and cook for about 4 minutes. Stir in spices, chili and garlic for about 30 seconds.

2. Stir in the remaining ingredients and lock the lid; set on manual high for 3 minutes.

3. When done, natural release the pressure and stir the mixture.

Crispy Feta with Zucchini Ribbons

Ingredients

Common Ingredients

- 1½ cup (340 g.) Feta Cheese
- ¼ cup (50 g.) Almond Flour
- 3 Medium Zucchinis
- 4 Egg Whites, beaten
- 1/8 cup (28 g.) Green Olives, Pitted and Sliced
- 1 tbsp. (15 g.) Minced Garlic
- 1 tsp. (5 g.) Dried Basil

Low fat version ingredients

- 1 tbsp. (45 ml) Olive Oil

High fat version ingredients

- 3 tbsp. (45 ml) Olive Oil

Nutrition

Prep: 20 min **Cook:** 15 min **Serves:** 3

High Fat Version	Low Fat Version
Kcal per serve: 500	**Kcal** per serve: 420
Fat: 42 g. (74%)	**Fat**: 33 g. (69%)
Protein: 23 g. (19%)	**Protein**: 23 g. (23%)
Carbs: 8 g (6%)	**Carbs**: 8 g (8%)

Zucchini Ribbons or 'zoodles' are all the rage right now and a great alternative to pasta.

Tip: This is a great warm weather salad when served cold!

Preparation

1. Cut feta cheese into thick cubes of about 2 inches. Dip the cheese cubes into the beaten eggs, then dredge in almond flour and refrigerate.
2. Heat oil in the Instant Pot on high and fry the cubes for about a minute until they turn crisp.
3. Place the crispy feta on paper towels and put aside.
4. Wash zucchini, form noodles using spiralizer or cut into ribbons using a peeler.
5. Place ½ cup water in the Pot. Add zucchini and cook in the Instant Pot for 2 minutes. Release pressure manually. Place cooked zucchini aside.
6. Dry the Pot and heat 3-4 tbsp. oil. Sauté garlic and add the zucchini. Add olives and season with salt and pepper.
7. Remove from heat and mix with the crispy feta.
8. Sprinkle basil and drizzle olive oil on top.

Vegetarian

Green Wraps

Ingredients

Common Ingredients

- ¼ head (200 g.) Romaine Lettuce
- 1 Cucumbers
- 4 Celery Stalks
- 1 Jalapeno Pepper
- Salt and black pepper to taste

Low fat version ingredients	High fat version ingredients
2 oz (60 g.) Cream Cheese	4 oz (120 g.) Cream Cheese
4 oz (120 g.) Avocado Slices	5 oz (150 g.) Avocado Slices
6 oz (180 g.) Raw Firm Tofu	4 oz (120 g.) Raw Firm Tofu
1/2 tbsp. Olive Oil	1 tbsp. Olive Oil

Nutrition

Prep: 10 min   **Cook:** 10 min   **Serves:** 4

High Fat Version
- Kcal per serve: 275
- Fat: 23 g. (79%)
- Protein: 8 g. (10%)
- Carbs: 9 g (5%)

Low Fat Version
- Kcal per serve: 200
- Fat: 14 g. (67%)
- Protein: 9 g. (17%)
- Carbs: 9 g (19%)

Fresh lettuce leaves filled with delicious ingredients make a quick and satisfying meal loved by children and adults alike. Enjoy these chilled crunchy wraps and cool off on a summer afternoon.

Tip: When selecting tofu, look for firm but spongy blocks that are free of harsh odours and discolorations.

Preparation

1. Julienne cucumbers and celery stalks into about 2-inch-long strips.
2. Chop tofu and sauté with olive oil in the Instant Pot for 5 minutes each side on high.
3. Carefully wash each leaf of the lettuce and lay them out on individual parchment papers. Spread about 2 tablespoons of cream cheese on each leaf.
4. Layer cucumbers, celery, avocado and jalapenos on top of the lettuce leaf.
5. Carefully roll each lettuce leaf into a wrap and secure with a toothpick.

Savoury Cauliflower Patties

Ingredients

Common Ingredients

- 3 Whole Eggs
- 1 Chilli Pepper, Finely Chopped
- ½ tsp. Garlic Powder
- Salt and ground pepper to taste

Low fat version ingredients	High fat version ingredients
3 cups (300 g.) Chopped Cauliflower	2 cups (200 g.) Chopped Cauliflower
¼ cup (50 ml) Olive Oil	¾ cup (150 ml) Olive Oil
¼ cup (50 g) non-fat Cheddar Cheese	¼ cup (50 g) Cheddar Cheese
¼ cup (50 g) non-fat Mozzarella Cheese	¼ cup (50 g) Whole Mozzarella Cheese

Nutrition

Prep: 5 min   **Cook:** 20 min   **Serves:** 4

High Fat Version
- **Kcal** per serve: 550
- **Fat:** 54 g. (87%)
- **Protein:** 13 g. (9%)
- **Carbs:** 5 g (4%)

Low Fat Version
- **Kcal** per serve: 225
- **Fat:** 17 g. (67%)
- **Protein:** 12 g. (21%)
- **Carbs:** 7 g (12%)

Take your burger game to the next level with these easy to make patties!

Tip: Make an extra batch and keep some in the freezer for a quick bite on a busy night!

Preparation

1. Cut the cauliflower into small florets, removing leaves and cutting out core. Put 1 cup of water in the Instant pot and set florets on a steamer basket to be placed on top of the trivet. Cook for 5 minutes and release pressure immediately.

2. Mash the steamed cauliflower and dry well with paper towels. Add the shredded cheeses, eggs, chilli, salt and pepper. Mix well and shape into slightly flat patties.

3. Heat oil in the Instant Pot. Shallow fry the patties until they are crisp on both sides.

Vegetarian

Chocolate Pudding

INGREDIENTS

Common Ingredients

- ¾ cup (150 ml) Coconut Milk
- ¼ (50 ml) cup Water
- 2 Egg Yolks
- 1/8 cup (16 g.) Baking Chocolate
- ¼ cup (28 g.) Cocoa Powder
- ¾ teaspoon (3.5 ml) Concentrated Stevia Extract
- 4-5 drops Vanilla Essence
- Pinch of Salt

Low fat version ingredients

- ½ cup (100 ml) Evaporated Milk

High fat version ingredients

- 1 cup (200 ml) Heavy Whipping Cream

NUTRITION

Prep: 15 min **Cook:** 25 min **Serves:** 4

High Fat Version	Low Fat Version
Kcal per serve: 280	Kcal per serve: 190
Fat: 26 g. (86%)	Fat: 15 g. (70%)
Protein: 5 g. (6%)	Protein: 5 g. (13%)
Carbs: 7 g (8%)	Carbs: 10 g (17%)

Who doesn't love chocolate pudding? This childhood favorite is a healthier version that won't ruin your diet!

Tip: You can add a sprinkle of chia seeds or toasted chopped nuts for a little crunch and protein boost!

PREPARATION

1. Combine coconut milk, water and whipping cream/evaporated milk with a whisk and heat until it begins to simmer. Remove from heat.
2. Chop cooking chocolate and mix until melted.
3. In a separate bowl, whisk together yolks, stevia, cocoa powder, vanilla and salt until well combined.
4. Add the egg mixture into the chocolate mixture until blended together uniformly.
5. Strain and pour into a 6-inch round baking dish. Cover tightly with aluminium foil.
6. Add 1½ cup of water into the Instant pot and place the baking dish on the trivet. Cook on low pressure for about 18 minutes. Naturally release pressure.
7. Uncover the dish and let it cool. Refrigerate for 3-4 hours before serving.

Tangy Berry Slice

Ingredients

Common Ingredients
- 1 cup (200 g.) Cottage Cheese
- ¼ cup (28 g.) Ground Pecans
- ¼ cup (28 g.) Whipped Cream
- ½ tsp. (2.5 g.) Stevia
- ½ cup (100 g.) Strawberries

Low fat version ingredients
- ¼ cup (28 g.) Light Butter

High fat version ingredients
- ¼ cup (28 g.) Unsalted Butter

Nutrition

Prep: 20 min   **Cook:** 15 min   **Serves:** 4

High Fat Version
- Kcal per serve: 220
- Fat: 18 g. (72%)
- Protein: 9 g. (19%)
- Carbs: 6 g (12%)

Low Fat Version
- Kcal per serve: 200
- Fat: 16 g. (69%)
- Protein: 9 g. (19%)
- Carbs: 6 g (12%)

This no fail layered dessert will instantly become a family favourite.

Tip: A coffee grinder makes a great nut grinder in a pinch!

Preparation

1. Heat butter in the Instant Pot and add pecans. Toss until they are well coated.
2. Divide this mixture into 3 and press down into individual ramekins.
3. Blend cheese with Stevia and puree until smooth.
4. Place cheese mixture on top of pecan crust.
5. Cover with fresh strawberry slices (or pureed strawberries) and top with whipped cream.
6. Refrigerate until ready to serve.

Dessert

Fluffy Eggy Muffins

INGREDIENTS

Egg Mix: Common Ingredients

- 4 eggs
- 1 tsp basil
- ½ tbsp. ground mustard
- ½ cup coconut yogurt
- ½ tsp cayenne pepper
- 1 tbsp baking powder
- 1 tbsp baking soda

The Filling: Low fat version

- 1 1/2 tbsp. extra virgin olive oil
- 2 tsp mix salt and freshly ground black pepper
- 2 jalapeno peppers, chopped
- ½ cup white onion, finely chopped
- 1 1/2 slices bacon

The Filling: High fat version

- 3 tbsp. extra virgin olive oil
- 2 tsp mix salt and freshly ground black pepper
- 2 jalapeno peppers, chopped
- ½ cup white onion, finely chopped
- 3 slices bacon

NUTRITION

Prep: 10 min   **Cook:** 25 min   **Serves:** 3

High Fat Version
- **Kcal** per serve: 470
- **Fat**: 39 g. (74%)
- **Protein**: 18 g. (16%)
- **Carbs**: 11 g (9%)

Low Fat Version
- **Kcal** per serve: 355
- **Fat**: 27 g. (68%)
- **Protein**: 16 g. (29%)
- **Carbs**: 11 g (12%)

Nothing says 'portable' more than these protein-packed muffins! Grab one on your way to work or school or anytime you need a quick snack!

Tip: Look for the freshest eggs you can. Make sure the 'sell by date' is within two weeks of purchase!

PREPARATION

1. Start by baking the bacon. Set it aside and crumble once cooled.
2. Add the olive oil to a pan over medium to low heat and sauté the onions, jalapenos, black pepper and salt until the onions brown. Don't increase the heat as this will make the onions burn and not brown well.
3. Break the eggs into a large mixing bowl and combine with the yogurt and once it's well blended, add the ground mustard, basil, cayenne, baking powder, baking soda, crumbled bacon and the cooked veggies.
4. Spray the muffin tins with olive oil cooking spray and divide the mixture evenly.
5. Add 1 cup of water to your instant pot and add a trivet; place the muffin pan on the trivet and lock lid; cook on high for 15 minutes and then let pressure come down naturally.
6. Broil until golden at the tops. Serve with hot sauce (if desired).

Spiced Gluten-Free Pancakes

NUTRITION

Prep: 10 min   **Cook:** 16 min   **Serves:** 3

Kcal per serve: 360   **Protein:** 13 g. (16%)
Fat: 33 g. (79%)   **Carbs:** 4 g (5%)

This is truly a superfood meal, packed with fiber, vitamins and minerals to keep you fuller longer.

Tip: Do some meal prep and put some in the freezer!

INGREDIENTS

- 1/3 cup almond flour
- ½ cup water
- ½ tsp. chili powder
- 1 serrano pepper minced
- 4 tbsp. coconut oil
- 3 tbsp. coconut cream
- ¼ tsp. turmeric powder
- 1 handful cilantro chopped
- 6 large eggs
- 1 tsp. salt plus
- ¼ tsp. black pepper
- ½ inch ginger, grated
- ½ red onion, chopped

PREPARATION

1. In a bowl, combine coconut milk, almond flour, and spices until well blended; stir in ginger, Serrano pepper, cilantro, and red onion until well combined.

2. Grease the interior of the instant pot with coconut oil; pour in the batter and seal the pot with vent closed; set pressure to low and cook for 30 minutes. Let pressure come down naturally.

3. Unlock lid and remove the giant pancake to a platter, cut into slices to serve.

4. Serve the crispy pancakes.

Dessert

Peanut Butter Cheesecake

Nutrition

Prep: 10 min **Cook:** 20 min **Serves:** 4

High Fat Version
- **Kcal** per serve: 480
- **Fat**: 43 g. (81%)
- **Protein**: 13 g. (11%)
- **Carbs**: 10 g (9%)

Low Fat Version
- **Kcal** per serve: 265
- **Fat**: 20 g. (64%)
- **Protein**: 16 g. (25%)
- **Carbs**: 7 g (11%)

A "Dulcet" dessert made with the indulgent mix of cheese and swirls of peanut butter for a deep, roasted nut flavor. The ultimate party dessert whips up this delicious cheesecake and impress your friends.

Tip: Look for no or low sodium peanut butter that has as few ingredients as possible with peanuts being the first ingredient.

Ingredients

Common Ingredients
- 1/8 cup (28 g.) Smooth Peanut Butter
- 2 Eggs
- ½ tsp. (2.5 g.) Stevia
- ½ tsp. (2.5 g.) Vanilla Extract

Topping Common Ingredients
- ½ cup (100 ml) Sour Cream
- 2 tbsp. (30 g.) Smooth Peanut Butter
- Pinch of Stevia

Low fat version ingredients
- 1 1/2 cups (300 g.) Cottage Cheese

High fat version ingredients
- 2 cups (400 g.) Cream Cheese

Preparation

1. Using a mixer, blend together cheese, peanut butter, eggs, stevia and vanilla extract.
2. Pour this mixture in a spring form pan and cover tightly with aluminium foil.
3. Add 2 cups of water in the Instant Pot. Place pan on the trivet. Cook on high pressure for 20 minutes. Release pressure naturally.
4. Cool to room temperature.
5. Mix together the topping ingredients and spread on top of the cheesecake and refrigerate.
6. Serve chilled.

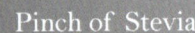

Almond Carrot Cake

Ingredients

- 4 large eggs
- ½ cup walnuts chopped
- ¾ cup almond flour
- 1 cup carrots shredded
- ¼ cup coconut oil
- 1 ½ tsp apple pie spice
- 1 tsp baking powder
- ½ cup heavy whipping cream
- 2/3 cup stevia

Nutrition

Prep: 10 min   **Cook:** 40 min   **Serves:** 4

Kcal per serve: 455   **Protein:** 10 g. (8%)
Fat: 44 g. (82%)   **Carbs:** 11 g (9%)

Light on effort but heavy on flavour, this delicious cake has earned its centuries-long reputation. It's soft and moist loaded with old-fashioned comfort, and the scrumptious walnuts make it even more special. Top the cake with a dollop of whipped cream for an extra flavour.

Preparation

1. Grease your 6-inch cake pan and set aside.

2. In a bowl, with the help of a hand mixer, mix together all ingredients until smooth and fluffy and then pour into the prepared pan; cover with foil.

3. Add two cups of water to your instant pot and insert a steamer rack; place the pan over the rack and lock lid; press "cake" button for 40 minutes and then let pressure come down on its own.

4. Remove cake from pot and let cool before icing.

Dessert

Recipe & Snack Nutrional Values

CHICKEN	Fat	Kcal/Srv	Srv	Fat (g)	Protein (g)	Carbs (g)
Roasted tandoori chicken	Low	662	4	50	49	4
Chicken Hainanese	Low	351	3	27	22	5
	High	535	3	45	28	5
Poached Chicken in Coconut and Lime Cream Sauce	Low	300	4	20	21	9
	High	425	4	33	24	9
Chicken Shawarma with Spicy Orange Sauce	Low	645	3	48	44	9
	High	725	3	60	37	9
Healthy Chicken Cacciatore	Low	600	3	43	44	7
	High	610	3	50	33	7
Stuffed Chicken	Low	545	3	40	39	6
	High	615	3	50	36	5
Tamarind & Lemongrass Braised Chicken	Low	445	4	32	28	9

SOUP & STEW	Fat	Kcal/Srv	Srv	Fat (g)	Protein (g)	Carbs (g)
Chicken and vegetable Soup	Low	445	4	33	28	9
	High	550	4	44	29	9
Spinach Chipotle Soup	Low	430	3	32	25	9
	High	550	3	46	25	9
Spicy Beef Cauliflower Soup	Low	400	4	26	32	8
Crab & Bamboo Egg Drop Soup	Low	325	3	21	27	7
	High	445	3	34	27	7
Hearty Keto Beef Stew	High	530	3	44	26	7
Minted Cream Soup	Low	310	4	23	18	9
	High	370	4	29	18	9
Asparagus and Celery Soup	Low	315	3	24	20	5
	High	439	3	39	19	5

TURKEY	Fat	Kcal/Srv	Srv	Fat (g)	Protein (g)	Carbs (g)
Juniper Citrus Turkey Leg Confit	Low	405	2	27	35	5
	High	640	2	53	35	5
Stuffed Turkey Thighs	Low	585	4	42	46	6
	High	568	4	47	33	5
Ground Turkey Stir Fry	Low	587	3	47	36	5
	High	590	3	49	30	7
Glazed Turkey Wings	Low	470	3	24	56	6
	High	590	3	47	38	4

LAMB	Fat	Kcal/Srv	Srv	Fat (g)	Protein (g)	Carbs (g)
Port Wine Lamb Shanks	High	495	3	34	37	10
Grilled Lamb & Veggies Bowl	Low	430	3	31	30	7
	High	510	3	40	30	7
Lamb leg with Gravy	Low	415	3	27	32	10
	High	570	3	45	32	10
Spicy Masala Lamb Chops	Low	463	4	27	49	6
	High	642	4	54	31	8
Lamb Ribs	Low	540	4	42	37	3
	High	590	4	48	37	3
Luscious Lamb Skewers	Low	320	4	12	49	4
	High	550	4	46	30	4

PORK	Fat	Kcal/Srv	Srv	Fat (g)	Protein (g)	Carbs (g)
Deonjang Pork Spare Ribs	Low	358	4	25	24	9
	High	448	4	35	24	9
Pork Luau	Low	585	2	40	56	0
Jamaican Jerk Pork Roast	Low	630	3	45	48	6
Avocado & Bacon Stuffed Peppers	High	420	3	34	21	9
Scrumptious Pork Chili	Low	430	3	30	30	10
	High	540	3	43	30	10
Tuscan Herbed Pork Chops	Low	485	4	32	42	6
	High	595	4	48	35	6

BEEF	Fat	Kcal/Srv	Srv	Fat (g)	Protein (g)	Carbs (g)
Balsamic & Rosemary Roast Beef	Low	570	3	42	39	8
Oatmeal Beef Meatballs	Low	330	4	20	30	7
	High	445	4	39	18	7
Italian Beef with Avocado	Low	500	3	35	37	9
	High	595	3	52	23	9
Spicy Beef Cauliflower Soup	Low	400	4	26	32	8
Ground Beef Skewers	Low	562	4	38	51	4
	High	600	4	48	39	4

DESSERT	Fat	Kcal/Srv	Srv	Fat (g)	Protein (g)	Carbs (g)
Fluffy Eggy Muffins	Low	355	3	27	16	11
	High	470	3	39	18	11
Spiced Gluten-Free Pancakes	High	360	3	33	13	4
Chocolate Pudding	Low	190	4	15	5	10
	High	280	4	26	5	7
Peanut Butter Cheesecake	Low	265	4	20	16	7
	High	480	4	43	13	10
Tangy Berry Slice	Low	200	4	16	9	6
	High	220	4	18	9	6
Almond Carrot Cake	High	455	4	44	10	11

VEGETARIAN	Fat	Kcal/Srv	Srv	Fat (g)	Protein (g)	Carbs (g)
Vegetable Hash	Low	210	2	14	14	8
	High	430	2	35	22	8
Scrambled Tofu	Low	300	2	20	24	7
	High	430	2	34	24	7
Coconut Cabbage	Low	265	2	18	15	10
	High	400	2	34	14	10
Crispy Feta & Zucchini Ribbons	Low	420	3	33	23	8
	High	500	3	42	23	8
Green Wraps	Low	200	4	14	9	9
	High	275	4	23	8	9
Egg Frittata	Low	255	3	19	14	6
	High	300	3	25	14	5
Savoury Cauliflower Patties	Low	225	4	17	12	7
	High	550	4	54	13	5

FISH/SEAFOOD	Fat	Kcal/Srv	Srv	Fat (g)	Protein (g)	Carbs (g)
Baked Cod	Low	395	3	28	29	9
	High	480	3	39	23	9
Lemon Kalamata Olive Salmon	Low	320	4	20	31	4
	High	440	4	34	30	3
Sweet Peppercorn Salmon	Low	395	4	28	32	4
	High	525	4	42	33	4
Creamy Chili Shrimp	Low	395	3	27	33	7
	High	555	3	45	33	7
Seafood Medley Stew	Low	460	3	36	26	8
	High	535	3	44	27	8

HIGH FAT SNACKS	Srv Wgt	Kcal/Srv	Fat (g)	Protein (g)	Carbs (g)
Pork rinds	1 oz (28.35g.)	165	10	18	0
Sunflower seeds	1 oz (28.35g.)	164	16	5	0
Laughing Cow cheese full fat	1 wedge	50	4	2	0
String cheese	2 oz (3 strings)	253	17	22	3
Jerky	1 oz (28.35g.)	120	8	9	3
Walnuts	1 oz (28.35g.)	203	19	4	4
Avocados	1 oz (28.35g.)	185	17	7	1
Hard-boiled egg (one unit)	2.5 oz (70g.)	130	10	7	1
Fat bomb: 25% butter, 25% coconut oil, 50% coconut meat	1 oz (28.35g.)	180	16	7	2

HIGH PROTEIN SNACKS	Srv Wgt	Kcal/Srv	Fat (g)	Protein (g)	Carbs (g)
Greek Yogurt (non-fat)	5 oz (140 g.)	85	1	15	4
Tuna can in water	6 oz (170 g.)	145	0	33	2
3 large egg whites (boiled or microwaved)	3 egg whites	51	0	10	1

Nutritional Values

Keto Meal Plan Schedules

Time to move onto offering a variety of meal prep eating schedules that will cater to a variety of Keto dieting needs. These may cover the needs for some people but not necessarily everyone's.

After you do your calculations for your required macros, you will have a caloric target and recommended fat %. With these two numbers, you will be able to select from the pages coming next which one fits the most to your needs.

For the sake of meal prepping, most of the times you must cook every recipe appearing in the schedule once every 2-week block (this is because cooking it once with the given servings in the recipe will cover all the times it appears on the schedule). Sometimes they will have to cook twice to cover all the required servings in a 2-week block. But all these is indicated in the meal summaries appearing before each schedule.

There are 1000 days' worth of Keto dieting, although for simplicity the first two weeks have been added, and the rest of the weekly schedules are available on this link below:

http://bit.ly/KetoMealPrepGuide

If you have any difficulties calculating or understanding macros, this guide will help you through it:

http://bit.ly/CalculateMacros

1125 Kcal (60% fat)

Day 1	Day 2	Day 3	Day 4	Day 5	Day 6	Day 7
Juniper Turkey (LF)* Beef Meatballs (LF) Sweet Salmon (LF)	Olive Salmon (LF) Scrambled Tofu (LF)* Olive Salmon (HF) 4 egg whites	Chicken Hainanese (LF) Asparagus Soup (LF) Glazed Turkey (LF)	Lamb Skewers (LF) Asparagus Soup (HF) Egg Drop Soup (LF) Laughing Cow cheese	Juniper Turkey (LF)* Beef Meatballs (LF) Sweet Salmon (LF)	Olive Salmon (LF) Scrambled Tofu (LF)* Olive Salmon (HF) 4 egg whites	Chicken Hainanese (LF) Asparagus Soup (LF) Glazed Turkey (LF)
Day 8	**Day 9**	**Day 10**	**Day 11**	**Day 12**	**Day 13**	**Day 14**
Lamb Skewers (LF) Asparagus Soup (HF) Egg Drop Soup (LF) Laughing Cow cheese	Juniper Turkey (LF)* Beef Meatballs (LF) Sweet Salmon (LF)	Olive Salmon (LF) Scrambled Tofu (LF)* Olive Salmon (HF) 4 egg whites	Chicken Hainanese (LF) Asparagus Soup (LF) Glazed Turkey (LF)	Juniper Turkey (LF)* Beef Meatballs (LF) Sweet Salmon (LF)	Lamb Skewers (LF) Asparagus Soup (HF) Egg Drop Soup (LF) Laughing Cow cheese	Olive Salmon (LF) Scrambled Tofu (LF)* Olive Salmon (HF) 4 egg whites

1250 Kcal (60% fat)

Day 1	Day 2	Day 3	Day 4	Day 5	Day 6	Day 7
Glazed Turkey (LF) Egg Frittata (HF) Chicken Hainanese (LF) Laughing Cow cheese 3 egg whites	Olive Salmon (LF) Vegetable Hash (HF) Lamb Skewers (LF) Avocados	Cauliflower Patties (LF) Juniper Turkey (LF)* Sweet Salmon (LF) 3 egg whites Pork rinds	Egg Frittata (LF) Lamb Ribs (LF) Asparagus Soup (LF) Tuna can 1 large egg white	Glazed Turkey (LF) Egg Frittata (HF) Chicken Hainanese (LF) Laughing Cow cheese 3 egg whites	Olive Salmon (LF) Scrambled Tofu (HF) Lamb Skewers (LF) Avocados	Cauliflower Patties (LF) Juniper Turkey (LF)* Sweet Salmon (LF) 3 egg whites Pork rinds
Day 8	**Day 9**	**Day 10**	**Day 11**	**Day 12**	**Day 13**	**Day 14**
Egg Frittata (LF) Lamb Ribs (LF) Asparagus Soup (LF) Tuna can 1 large egg white	Glazed Turkey (LF) Egg Frittata (HF) Chicken Hainanese (LF) Laughing Cow cheese 3 egg whites	Olive Salmon (LF) Vegetable Hash (HF) Lamb Skewers (LF) Avocados	Cauliflower Patties (LF) Juniper Turkey (LF)* Sweet Salmon (LF) 3 egg whites Pork rinds	Olive Salmon (LF) Scrambled Tofu (HF) Lamb Skewers (LF) Avocados	Egg Frittata (LF) Lamb Ribs (LF) Asparagus Soup (LF) Tuna can 1 large egg white	Cauliflower Patties (LF) Juniper Turkey (LF)* Sweet Salmon (LF) 3 egg whites Pork rinds

1250 Kcal (66% fat)

Day 1	Day 2	Day 3	Day 4	Day 5	Day 6	Day 7
Minted Soup (HF) Sweet Salmon (HF) Olive Salmon (LF) 3 egg whites	Olive Salmon (HF) Scrambled Tofu (LF)* Sweet Salmon (LF) Hard boiled egg	Egg Drop Soup (HF) Spiced Pancakes (HF) Asparagus Soup (LF) Tuna can	Stuffed Chicken (LF) Chicken Hainanese (LF) Egg Drop Soup (LF) Laughing Cow cheese	Minted Soup (HF) Sweet Salmon (HF) Olive Salmon (LF) 3 egg whites	Olive Salmon (HF) Scrambled Tofu (LF)* Sweet Salmon (LF) Hard boiled egg	Egg Drop Soup (HF) Spiced Pancakes (HF) Asparagus Soup (LF) Tuna can
Day 8	**Day 9**	**Day 10**	**Day 11**	**Day 12**	**Day 13**	**Day 14**
Stuffed Chicken (LF) Chicken Hainanese (LF) Egg Drop Soup (LF) Laughing Cow cheese	Minted Soup (HF) Sweet Salmon (HF) Olive Salmon (LF) 3 egg whites	Olive Salmon (HF) Scrambled Tofu (LF)* Sweet Salmon (LF) Hard boiled egg	Egg Drop Soup (HF) Spiced Pancakes (HF) Asparagus Soup (LF) Tuna can	Minted Soup (HF) Sweet Salmon (HF) Olive Salmon (LF) 3 egg whites	Stuffed Chicken (LF) Chicken Hainanese (LF) Egg Drop Soup (LF) Laughing Cow cheese	Olive Salmon (HF) Scrambled Tofu (LF)* Sweet Salmon (LF) Hard boiled egg

1375 Kcal (59% fat)

Day 1	Day 2	Day 3	Day 4	Day 5	Day 6	Day 7
Spiced Pancakes (HF) Egg Frittata (HF) Chicken Hainanese (LF) Tuna can 1 egg white Laughing Cow cheese	Olive Salmon (HF) Lamb Skewers (LF) Sweet Salmon (LF) Fat bomb Greek Yogurt	Glazed Turkey (HF) Asparagus Soup (LF) Egg Frittata (LF) 5 egg whites Tuna can	Olive Salmon (LF) Juniper Turkey(LF)* Sweet Salmon (LF) String cheese	Spiced Pancakes (HF) Egg Frittata (HF) Chicken Hainanese (LF) Tuna can 1 egg white Laughing Cow cheese	Olive Salmon (HF) Lamb Skewers (LF) Sweet Salmon (LF) Fat bomb Greek Yogurt	Glazed Turkey (HF) Asparagus Soup (LF) Egg Frittata (LF) 5 egg whites Tuna can
Day 8	**Day 9**	**Day 10**	**Day 11**	**Day 12**	**Day 13**	**Day 14**
Olive Salmon (LF) Juniper Turkey(LF)* Sweet Salmon (LF) String cheese	Spiced Pancakes (HF) Egg Frittata (HF) Chicken Hainanese (LF) Tuna can 1 egg white Laughing Cow cheese	Olive Salmon (HF) Lamb Skewers (LF) Sweet Salmon (LF) Fat bomb Greek Yogurt	Olive Salmon (LF) Juniper Turkey(LF)* Sweet Salmon (LF) String cheese	Turkey (HF) Asparagus Soup (LF) Egg Frittata (LF) 5 egg whites Tuna can	Olive Salmon (HF) Lamb Skewers (LF) Sweet Salmon (LF) Fat bomb Greek Yogurt	Olive Salmon (LF) Juniper Turkey(LF)* Sweet Salmon (LF) String cheese

1375 Kcal (65% fat)

Day 1	Day 2	Day 3	Day 4	Day 5	Day 6	Day 7
Poached Chicken (LF) Turkey Thighs (HF) Olive Salmon (HF) Tuna can	Lamb Ribs (LF) Braised Chicken (LF) Juniper Turkey (LF)*	Chicken Cacciatore (LF) Chicken Hainanese (LF) Asparagus Soup (LF) Laughing Cow cheese 4 egg whites	Glazed Turkey (HF) Chili Shrimp (LF) Egg Drop Soup (LF) Laughing Cow cheese	Poached Chicken (LF) Turkey Thighs (HF) Olive Salmon (HF) Tuna can	Lamb Ribs (LF) Braised Chicken (LF) Juniper Turkey (LF)*	Chicken Cacciatore (LF) Chicken Hainanese (LF) Asparagus Soup (LF) Laughing Cow cheese 4 egg whites
Day 8	**Day 9**	**Day 10**	**Day 11**	**Day 12**	**Day 13**	**Day 14**
Glazed Turkey (HF) Chili Shrimp (LF) Egg Drop Soup (LF) Laughing Cow cheese	Poached Chicken (LF) Turkey Thighs (HF) Olive Salmon (HF) Tuna can	Lamb Ribs (LF) Braised Chicken (LF) Juniper Turkey (LF)*	Chicken Cacciatore (LF) Chicken Hainanese (LF) Asparagus Soup (LF) Laughing Cow cheese 4 egg whites	Poached Chicken (LF) Turkey Thighs (HF) Olive Salmon (HF) Tuna can	Glazed Turkey (HF) Chili Shrimp (LF) Egg Drop Soup (LF) Laughing Cow cheese	Lamb Ribs (LF) Braised Chicken (LF) Juniper Turkey (LF)*

1375 Kcal (70% fat)

Day 1	Day 2	Day 3	Day 4	Day 5	Day 6	Day 7
Pork Spare Ribs (HF) Luscious Lamb Skewers (HF) Sweet Salmon (LF)	Poached Chicken (HF) Lamb Ribs (LF) Scrambled Tofu (HF)*	Chili Shrimp (LF) Glazed Turkey (HF) Egg Frittata (HF) Avocados	Chicken Hainanese (HF) Egg Drop Soup (LF) Grilled Lamb (HF)	Pork Spare Ribs (HF) Luscious Lamb Skewers (HF) Sweet Salmon (LF)	Poached Chicken (HF) Lamb Ribs (LF) Scrambled Tofu (HF)*	Chili Shrimp (LF) Glazed Turkey (HF) Egg Frittata (HF) Avocados
Day 8	**Day 9**	**Day 10**	**Day 11**	**Day 12**	**Day 13**	**Day 14**
Chicken Hainanese (HF) Egg Drop Soup (LF) Grilled Lamb (HF)	Pork Spare Ribs (HF) Luscious Lamb Skewers (HF) Sweet Salmon (LF)	Poached Chicken (HF) Lamb Ribs (LF) Scrambled Tofu (HF)*	Chili Shrimp (LF) Glazed Turkey (HF) Egg Frittata (HF) Avocados	Pork Spare Ribs (HF) Luscious Lamb Skewers (HF) Sweet Salmon (LF)	Chicken Hainanese (HF) Egg Drop Soup (LF) Grilled Lamb (HF)	Poached Chicken (HF) Lamb Ribs (LF) Scrambled Tofu (HF)*

Meal Plans

1500 Kcal (60% fat)

Day 1	Day 2	Day 3	Day 4	Day 5	Day 6	Day 7
Braised Chicken (LF) Lamb Ribs (HF) Beef Meatballs (LF) Tuna can	Pork Spare Ribs (LF) Tandoori chicken (LF) Masala Lamb (LF) 2 egg whites	Seafood Stew (LF) Glazed Turkey (LF) Asparagus Soup (HF) Tuna can	Jerk Pork Roast (LF) Egg Frittata (HF) Grilled Lamb (LF) Tuna can) 1 egg white	Braised Chicken (LF) Lamb Ribs (HF) Beef Meatballs (LF) Tuna can	Pork Spare Ribs (LF) Tandoori chicken (LF) Masala Lamb (LF) 2 egg whites	Seafood Stew (LF) Glazed Turkey (LF) Asparagus Soup (HF) Tuna can
Day 8	**Day 9**	**Day 10**	**Day 11**	**Day 12**	**Day 13**	**Day 14**
Jerk Pork Roast (LF) Egg Frittata (HF) Grilled Lamb (LF) Tuna can) 1 egg white	Braised Chicken (LF) Lamb Ribs (HF) Beef Meatballs (LF) Tuna can	Pork Spare Ribs (LF) Tandoori chicken (LF) Masala Lamb (LF) 2 egg whites	Seafood Stew (LF) Glazed Turkey (LF) Asparagus Soup (HF) Tuna can	Braised Chicken (LF) Lamb Ribs (HF) Beef Meatballs (LF) Tuna can	Jerk Pork Roast (LF) Egg Frittata (HF) Grilled Lamb (LF) Tuna can) 1 egg white	Pork Spare Ribs (LF) Tandoori chicken (LF) Masala Lamb (LF) 2 egg whites

1500 Kcal (65% fat)

Day 1	Day 2	Day 3	Day 4	Day 5	Day 6	Day 7
Grilled Lamb (HF) Chicken Hainanese (LF) Asparagus Soup (LF) Avocados Tuna can	Herbed Pork Chops (LF) Olive Salmon (HF) Beef Meatballs (HF) 6egg whites Laughing Cow cheese	Jerk Pork Roast (LF) Chili Shrimp (LF) Grilled Lamb(LF) Laughing Cow cheese	Lamb Ribs (LF) Scrambled Tofu (HF) Sweet Salmon (LF) Greek Yogurt Laughing Cow cheese	Grilled Lamb (HF) Chicken Hainanese (LF) Asparagus Soup (LF) Avocados Tuna can	Herbed Pork Chops (LF) Olive Salmon (HF) Beef Meatballs (HF) 6 egg whites Laughing Cow cheese	Jerk Pork Roast (LF) Chili Shrimp (LF) Grilled Lamb(LF) Laughing Cow cheese
Day 8	**Day 9**	**Day 10**	**Day 11**	**Day 12**	**Day 13**	**Day 14**
Lamb Ribs (LF) Vegetable Hash (HF) Or Crispy Feta Ribbons (LF) Sweet Salmon (LF) Greek Yogurt Laughing Cow cheese	Grilled Lamb (HF) Chicken Hainanese (LF) Asparagus Soup (LF) Avocados Tuna can	Herbed Pork Chops (LF) Olive Salmon (HF) Beef Meatballs (HF) 6egg whites Laughing Cow cheese	Jerk Pork Roast (LF) Chili Shrimp (LF) Grilled Lamb(LF) Laughing Cow cheese	Lamb Ribs (LF) Scrambled Tofu (HF) Sweet Salmon (LF) Greek Yogurt Laughing Cow cheese	Herbed Pork Chops (LF) Olive Salmon (HF) Beef Meatballs (HF) 6 egg whites Laughing Cow cheese	Lamb Ribs (LF) Vegetable Hash (HF) Or Crispy Feta Ribbons (LF) Sweet Salmon (LF) Greek Yogurt Laughing Cow cheese

1500 Kcal (70% fat)

Day 1	Day 2	Day 3	Day 4	Day 5	Day 6	Day 7
Coconut Cabbage (HF)* Pork Luau (LF)* Minted Soup (LF) Avocados Laughing Cow cheese	Scrambled Tofu (LF)* Lamb Ribs (HF) Pork Spare Ribs (HF) Fat bomb	Stuffed Peppers (HF) Stuffed Chicken (LF) Asparagus Soup (HF) Laughing Cow cheese 3 egg whites	Port Wine Lamb (HF) Glazed Turkey (HF) Egg Frittata (LF) Avocados	Coconut Cabbage (HF)* Pork Luau (LF)* Minted Soup (LF) Avocados Laughing Cow cheese	Scrambled Tofu (LF)* Lamb Ribs (HF) Pork Spare Ribs (HF) Fat bomb	Stuffed Peppers (HF) Stuffed Chicken (LF) Asparagus Soup (HF) Laughing Cow cheese 3 egg whites
Day 8	**Day 9**	**Day 10**	**Day 11**	**Day 12**	**Day 13**	**Day 14**
Port Wine Lamb (HF) Glazed Turkey (HF) Egg Frittata (LF) Avocados	Coconut Cabbage (HF)* Pork Luau (LF)* Minted Soup (LF) Avocados Laughing Cow cheese	Scrambled Tofu (LF)* Lamb Ribs (HF) Pork Spare Ribs (HF) Fat bomb	Stuffed Peppers (HF) Stuffed Chicken (LF) Asparagus Soup (HF) Laughing Cow cheese 3 egg whites	Coconut Cabbage (HF)* Pork Luau (LF)* Minted Soup (LF) Avocados Laughing Cow cheese	Port Wine Lamb (HF) Glazed Turkey (HF) Egg Frittata (LF) Avocados	Scrambled Tofu (LF)* Lamb Ribs (HF) Pork Spare Ribs (HF) Fat bomb

1625 Kcal (60% fat)

Day 1	Day 2	Day 3	Day 4	Day 5	Day 6	Day 7
Masala Lamb (LF) Spicy Beef Soup (LF) Tandoori chicken (LF)	Chicken Soup (LF) Turkey Thighs (LF) Sweet Salmon (LF) Tuna can Laughing Cow cheese	Baked Cod (LF) Glazed Turkey (LF) Stuffed Chicken (HF) Sunflower seeds Tuna can	Chicken Hainanese (LF) Seafood Stew (LF) Chicken Hainanese (HF) Tuna can	Masala Lamb (LF) Spicy Beef Soup (LF) Tandoori chicken (LF)	Chicken Soup (LF) Turkey Thighs (LF) Sweet Salmon (LF) Tuna can Laughing Cow cheese	Baked Cod (LF) Glazed Turkey (LF) Stuffed Chicken (HF) Sunflower seeds Tuna can
Day 8	**Day 9**	**Day 10**	**Day 11**	**Day 12**	**Day 13**	**Day 14**
Chicken Hainanese (LF) Seafood Stew (LF) Chicken Hainanese (HF) Tuna can	Masala Lamb (LF) Spicy Beef Soup (LF) Tandoori chicken (LF)	Chicken Soup (LF) Turkey Thighs (LF) Sweet Salmon (LF) Tuna can	Baked Cod (LF) Glazed Turkey (LF) Stuffed Chicken (HF) Sunflower seeds Tuna can	Masala Lamb (LF) Spicy Beef Soup (LF) Tandoori chicken (LF)	Chicken Hainanese (LF) Seafood Stew (LF) Chicken Hainanese (HF) Tuna can	Chicken Soup (LF) Turkey Thighs (LF) Sweet Salmon (LF) Tuna can Laughing Cow cheese

1625 Kcal (65% fat)

Day 1	Day 2	Day 3	Day 4	Day 5	Day 6	Day 7
Minted Cream Soup (HF) Beef Skewers (LF) Herbed Pork Chops (LF) Fat bomb Laughing Cow cheese	Olive Salmon (LF) Green Wraps (HF) Berry Slice (LF) Olive Salmon (HF) Pork rinds	Lamb with Gravy (LF) Jerk Pork Roast (LF) Turkey Stir Fry (LF) 1 egg white	Chicken Cacciatore (LF) Italian Beef (LF) Stuffed Chicken (LF)	Minted Cream Soup (HF) Beef Skewers (LF) Herbed Pork Chops (LF) Fat bomb Laughing Cow cheese	Olive Salmon (LF) Green Wraps (HF) Berry Slice (LF) Olive Salmon (HF) Pork rinds	Lamb with Gravy (LF) Jerk Pork Roast (LF) Turkey Stir Fry (LF) 1 egg white
Day 8	**Day 9**	**Day 10**	**Day 11**	**Day 12**	**Day 13**	**Day 14**
Chicken Cacciatore (LF) Italian Beef (LF) Stuffed Chicken (LF)	Minted Cream Soup (HF) Beef Skewers (LF) Herbed Pork Chops (LF) Fat bomb Laughing Cow cheese	Olive Salmon (LF) Green Wraps (HF) Berry Slice (LF) Olive Salmon (HF) Pork rinds	Lamb with Gravy (LF) Jerk Pork Roast (LF) Turkey Stir Fry (LF) 1 egg white	Minted Cream Soup (HF) Beef Skewers (LF) Herbed Pork Chops (LF) Fat bomb Laughing Cow cheese	Chicken Cacciatore (LF) Italian Beef (LF) Stuffed Chicken (LF)	Olive Salmon (LF) Green Wraps (HF) Berry Slice (LF) Olive Salmon (HF) Pork rinds

1625 Kcal (70% fat)

Day 1	Day 2	Day 3	Day 4	Day 5	Day 6	Day 7
Poached Chicken (LF) Masala Lamb (HF) Tandoori chicken (LF) Laughing Cow cheese	Pork Spare Ribs (LF) Juniper Turkey (HF)* Turkey Thighs (HF) 3 egg whites	Egg Drop Soup (LF) Chipotle Soup (HF) Glazed Turkey (HF) 1 boiled egg Laughing Cow cheese	Port Wine Lamb (HF) Stuffed Chicken (LF) Asparagus Soup (HF) 1 boiled egg Laughing Cow cheese	Poached Chicken (LF) Masala Lamb (HF) Tandoori chicken (LF) Laughing Cow cheese	Pork Spare Ribs (LF) Juniper Turkey (HF)* Turkey Thighs (HF) 3 egg whites	Egg Drop Soup (LF) Chipotle Soup (HF) Glazed Turkey (HF) 1 boiled egg Laughing Cow cheese
Day 8	**Day 9**	**Day 10**	**Day 11**	**Day 12**	**Day 13**	**Day 14**
Port Wine Lamb (HF) Stuffed Chicken (LF) Asparagus Soup (HF) 1 boiled egg Laughing Cow cheese	Poached Chicken (LF) Masala Lamb (HF) Tandoori chicken (LF) Laughing Cow cheese	Pork Spare Ribs (LF) Juniper Turkey (HF)* Turkey Thighs (HF) 3 egg whites	Egg Drop Soup (LF) Chipotle Soup (HF) Glazed Turkey (HF) 1 boiled egg Laughing Cow cheese	Poached Chicken (LF) Masala Lamb (HF) Tandoori chicken (LF) Laughing Cow cheese	Port Wine Lamb (HF) Stuffed Chicken (LF) Asparagus Soup (HF) 1 boiled egg Laughing Cow cheese	Pork Spare Ribs (LF) Juniper Turkey (HF)* Turkey Thighs (HF) 3 egg whites

1750 Kcal (63% fat)

Day 1	Day 2	Day 3	Day 4	Day 5	Day 6	Day 7
Chicken Hainanese (LF) Glazed Turkey (LF) Chili Shrimp (LF) Spiced Pancakes (HF) Pork rinds	Sweet Salmon (LF) Spicy Beef Soup (LF) Berry Slice (HF) Olive Salmon (HF) Sunflower seeds Tuna can	Egg Drop Soup (HF) Grilled Lamb (LF) Asparagus Soup (HF) Pork rinds Tuna can Laughing Cow cheese	Lamb Ribs (LF) Cauliflower Patties (LF) Chocolate Pudding (LF) Pork Luau (LF) Jerky Tuna can Laughing Cow cheese	Chicken Hainanese (LF) Glazed Turkey (LF) Chili Shrimp (LF) Spiced Pancakes (HF) Pork rinds	Sweet Salmon (LF) Spicy Beef Soup (LF) Berry Slice (HF) Olive Salmon (HF) Sunflower seeds Tuna can	Lamb Ribs (LF) Cauliflower Patties (LF) Chocolate Pudding (LF) Pork Luau (LF) Jerky Tuna can Laughing Cow cheese
Day 8	**Day 9**	**Day 10**	**Day 11**	**Day 12**	**Day 13**	**Day 14**
Egg Drop Soup (HF) Grilled Lamb (LF) Asparagus Soup (HF) Pork rinds Tuna can Laughing Cow cheese	Lamb Ribs (LF) Cauliflower Patties (LF) Chocolate Pudding (LF) Pork Luau (LF) Jerky Tuna can Laughing Cow cheese	Chicken Hainanese (LF) Glazed Turkey (LF) Chili Shrimp (LF) Spiced Pancakes (HF) Pork rinds	Sweet Salmon (LF) Spicy Beef Soup (LF) Berry Slice (HF) Olive Salmon (HF) Sunflower seeds Tuna can	Egg Drop Soup (HF) Grilled Lamb (LF) Asparagus Soup (HF) Pork rinds Tuna can Laughing Cow cheese	Lamb Ribs (LF) Cauliflower Patties (LF) Chocolate Pudding (LF) Pork Luau (LF) Jerky Tuna can Laughing Cow cheese	Sweet Salmon (LF) Spicy Beef Soup (LF) Berry Slice (HF) Olive Salmon (HF) Sunflower seeds Tuna can

1750 Kcal (67% fat)

Day 1	Day 2	Day 3	Day 4	Day 5	Day 6	Day 7
Braised Chicken (LF) Beef Meatballs (LF) Turkey Thighs (LF) Sunflower seeds Laughing Cow cheese 2 egg whites	Poached Chicken (HF) Lamb Ribs (HF) Herbed Pork Chops (LF) String cheese	Stuffed Chicken (LF) Chili Shrimp (HF) Chicken Cacciatore (LF) 3 egg whites	Pork Chili (LF) Asparagus Soup (HF) Jerk Pork Roast (LF) Pork rinds Laughing Cow cheese Greek Yogurt	Braised Chicken (LF) Beef Meatballs (LF) Turkey Thighs (LF) Sunflower seeds Laughing Cow cheese 2 egg whites	Poached Chicken (HF) Lamb Ribs (HF) Herbed Pork Chops (LF) String cheese	Stuffed Chicken (LF) Chili Shrimp (HF) Chicken Cacciatore (LF) 3 egg whites
Day 8	**Day 9**	**Day 10**	**Day 11**	**Day 12**	**Day 13**	**Day 14**
Pork Chili (LF) Asparagus Soup (HF) Jerk Pork Roast (LF) Pork rinds Laughing Cow cheese Greek Yogurt	Braised Chicken (LF) Beef Meatballs (LF) Turkey Thighs (LF) Sunflower seeds Laughing Cow cheese 2 egg whites	Stuffed Chicken (LF) Chili Shrimp (HF) Chicken Cacciatore (LF) 3 egg whites	Poached Chicken (HF) Lamb Ribs (HF) Herbed Pork Chops (LF) String cheese	Braised Chicken (LF) Beef Meatballs (LF) Turkey Thighs (LF) Sunflower seeds Laughing Cow cheese 2 egg whites	Pork Chili (LF) Asparagus Soup (HF) Jerk Pork Roast (LF) Pork rinds Laughing Cow cheese Greek Yogurt	Poached Chicken (HF) Lamb Ribs (HF) Herbed Pork Chops (LF) String cheese

Meal Plans

1750 Kcal (73% fat)

Day 1	Day 2	Day 3	Day 4	Day 5	Day 6	Day 7
Turkey Stir Fry (LF) Lamb with Gravy (HF) Chipotle Soup (HF) Laughing Cow cheese	Sweet Salmon (HF) Beef Meatballs (LF) Cauliflower Patties (HF) Walnuts Sunflower seeds Greek Yogurt	Baked Cod (HF) Spiced Pancakes (HF) Asparagus Soup (LF) Chicken Hainanese (LF) Sunflower seeds Laughing Cow cheese 3 egg whites	Beef Skewers (HF) Pork Spare Ribs (HF) Chicken Soup (HF) Sunflower seeds	Turkey Stir Fry (LF) Lamb with Gravy (HF) Chipotle Soup (HF) Laughing Cow cheese	Sweet Salmon (HF) Beef Meatballs (LF) Cauliflower Patties (HF) Walnuts Sunflower seeds Greek Yogurt	Baked Cod (HF) Spiced Pancakes (HF) Asparagus Soup (LF) Chicken Hainanese (LF) Sunflower seeds Laughing Cow cheese 3 egg whites

Day 8	Day 9	Day 10	Day 11	Day 12	Day 13	Day 14
Beef Skewers (HF) Pork Spare Ribs (HF) Chicken Soup (HF) Sunflower seeds	Sweet Salmon (HF) Beef Meatballs (LF) Cauliflower Patties (LF) Walnuts Sunflower seeds Greek Yogurt	Beef Skewers (HF) Pork Spare Ribs (HF) Chicken Soup (HF) Sunflower seeds	Turkey Stir Fry (LF) Lamb with Gravy (HF) Chipotle Soup (HF) Laughing Cow cheese	Sweet Salmon (HF) Beef Meatballs (LF) Cauliflower Patties (HF) Walnuts Sunflower seeds Greek Yogurt	Baked Cod (HF) Spiced Pancakes (HF) Asparagus Soup (LF) Chicken Hainanese (LF) Sunflower seeds Laughing Cow cheese 3 egg whites	Beef Skewers (HF) Pork Spare Ribs (HF) Chicken Soup (HF) Sunflower seeds

1825 Kcal (66% fat)

Day 1	Day 2	Day 3	Day 4	Day 5	Day 6	Day 7
Turkey Thighs (LF) Lamb Ribs (LF) Chicken Soup (HF) Jerky 3 egg whites	Herbed Pork Chops (HF) Beef Skewers (LF) Olive Salmon (HF) Chocolate Pudding (LF) 3 egg whites	Chicken Cacciatore (LF) Jerk Pork Roast (LF) Seafood Stew (HF) Greek Yogurt	Chicken Hainanese (HF) Chipotle Soup (LF) Stuffed Chicken (HF) Pork rinds Laughing Cow cheese Tuna can	Turkey Thighs (LF) Lamb Ribs (LF) Chicken Soup (HF) Jerky 3 egg whites	Herbed Pork Chops (HF) Beef Skewers (LF) Olive Salmon (HF) Chocolate Pudding (LF) 3 egg whites	Chicken Hainanese (HF) Chipotle Soup (LF) Stuffed Chicken (HF) Pork rinds Laughing Cow cheese Tuna can

Day 8	Day 9	Day 10	Day 11	Day 12	Day 13	Day 14
Chicken Cacciatore (LF) Jerk Pork Roast (LF) Seafood Stew (HF) Greek Yogurt	Turkey Thighs (LF) Lamb Ribs (LF) Chicken Soup (HF) Jerky 3 egg whites	Chicken Hainanese (HF) Chipotle Soup (LF) Stuffed Chicken (HF) Pork rinds Laughing Cow cheese Tuna can	Herbed Pork Chops (HF) Beef Skewers (LF) Olive Salmon (HF) Chocolate Pudding (LF) 3 egg whites	Turkey Thighs (LF) Lamb Ribs (LF) Chicken Soup (HF) Jerky 3 egg whites	Chicken Cacciatore (LF) Jerk Pork Roast (LF) Seafood Stew (HF) Greek Yogurt	Herbed Pork Chops (HF) Beef Skewers (LF) Olive Salmon (HF) Chocolate Pudding (LF) 3 egg whites

1825 Kcal (73% fat)

Day 1	Day 2	Day 3	Day 4	Day 5	Day 6	Day 7
Lamb Skewers (HF) Poached (HF) Turkey Thighs (HF) Peanut Cheesecake (LF)	Chicken Shawarma (HF) Grilled Lamb (HF) Turkey Stir Fry (HF)	Tandoori chicken (LF) Pork Spare Ribs (HF) Cauliflower Patties (HF) Jerky Greek Yogurt	Pork Chili (HF) Chicken Cacciatore (HF) Chili Shrimp (HF) Boiled egg	Lamb Skewers (HF) Poached (HF) Turkey Thighs (HF) Peanut Cheesecake (LF)	Chicken Shawarma (HF) Grilled Lamb (HF) Turkey Stir Fry (HF)	Tandoori chicken (LF) Pork Spare Ribs (HF) Cauliflower Patties (HF) Jerky Greek Yogurt

Day 8	Day 9	Day 10	Day 11	Day 12	Day 13	Day 14
Pork Chili (HF) Chicken Cacciatore (HF) Chili Shrimp (HF) Boiled egg	Lamb Skewers (HF) Poached (HF) Turkey Thighs (HF) Peanut Cheesecake (LF)	Tandoori chicken (LF) Pork Spare Ribs (HF) Cauliflower Patties (HF) Jerky Greek Yogurt	Chicken Shawarma (HF) Grilled Lamb (HF) Turkey Stir Fry (HF)	Pork Chili (HF) Chicken Cacciatore (HF) Chili Shrimp (HF) Boiled egg	Lamb Skewers (HF) Poached (HF) Turkey Thighs (HF) Peanut Cheesecake (LF)	Tandoori chicken (LF) Pork Spare Ribs (HF) Cauliflower Patties (HF) Jerky Greek Yogurt

2000 Kcal (66% fat)

Day 1	Day 2	Day 3	Day 4	Day 5	Day 6	Day 7
Herbed Pork Chops (LF) Beef Meatballs (HF) Lamb Ribs (LF) Berry Slice (HF) String cheese 4 egg whites	Chicken Cacciatore (LF) Jerk Pork Roast (LF) Balsamic Beef (LF) Fat bomb 3 egg whites	Chicken Soup (HF) Turkey Thighs (LF) Sweet Salmon (HF) Jerky Pork rinds 3 egg whites	Egg Drop Soup (HF) Grilled Lamb (LF) Glazed Turkey(LF) Walnuts Avocados 3 egg whites Laughing Cow cheese	Herbed Pork Chops (LF) Beef Meatballs (HF) Lamb Ribs (LF) Berry Slice (HF) String cheese 4 egg whites	Chicken Cacciatore (LF) Jerk Pork Roast (LF) Balsamic Beef (LF) Fat bomb 3 egg whites	Chicken Soup (HF) Turkey Thighs (LF) Sweet Salmon (HF) Jerky Pork rinds 3 egg whites

Day 8	Day 9	Day 10	Day 11	Day 12	Day 13	Day 14
Egg Drop Soup (HF) Grilled Lamb (LF) Glazed Turkey(LF) Walnuts Avocados 3 egg whites Laughing Cow cheese	Herbed Pork Chops (LF) Beef Meatballs (HF) Lamb Ribs (LF) Berry Slice (HF) String cheese 4 egg whites	Chicken Soup (HF) Turkey Thighs (LF) Sweet Salmon (HF) Jerky Pork rinds 3 egg whites	Chicken Cacciatore (LF) Jerk Pork Roast (LF) Balsamic Beef (LF) Fat bomb 3 egg whites	Egg Drop Soup (HF) Grilled Lamb (LF) Glazed Turkey(LF) Walnuts Avocados 3 egg whites Laughing Cow cheese	Herbed Pork Chops (LF) Beef Meatballs (HF) Lamb Ribs (LF) Berry Slice (HF) String cheese 4 egg whites	Chicken Soup (HF) Turkey Thighs (LF) Sweet Salmon (HF) Jerky Pork rinds 3 egg whites

2000 Kcal (73% fat)

Day 1	Day 2	Day 3	Day 4	Day 5	Day 6	Day 7
Stuffed Chicken (HF) Lamb with Gravy (HF) Chili Shrimp (HF) Fat bomb	Masala Lamb Chops (HF) Cauliflower Patties (HF) Sweet Salmon (HF) String cheese Greek Yogurt Laughing Cow cheese	Chicken Hainanese (HF) Beef Stew (HF) Seafood Stew (HF) Berry Slice (HF) Pork rinds 1 egg white	Chicken Soup (HF) Lamb Ribs (HF) Chocolate Pudding (LF) Beef Skewers (HF) Sunflower seeds	Stuffed Chicken (HF) Lamb with Gravy (HF) Chili Shrimp (HF) Fat bomb	Masala Lamb Chops (HF) Cauliflower Patties (HF) Sweet Salmon (HF) String cheese Greek Yogurt Laughing Cow cheese	Chicken Hainanese (HF) Beef Stew (HF) Seafood Stew (HF) Berry Slice (HF) Pork rinds 1 egg white
Day 8	**Day 9**	**Day 10**	**Day 11**	**Day 12**	**Day 13**	**Day 14**
Chicken Soup (HF) Lamb Ribs (HF) Chocolate Pudding (LF) Beef Skewers (HF) Sunflower seeds	Masala Lamb Chops (HF) Cauliflower Patties (HF) Sweet Salmon (HF) String cheese Greek Yogurt Laughing Cow cheese	Chicken Soup (HF) Lamb Ribs (HF) Chocolate Pudding (LF) Beef Skewers (HF) Sunflower seeds	Chicken Hainanese (HF) Beef Stew (HF) Seafood Stew (HF) Berry Slice (HF) Pork rinds 1 egg white	Stuffed Chicken (HF) Lamb with Gravy (HF) Chili Shrimp (HF) Fat bomb	Masala Lamb Chops (HF) Cauliflower Patties (HF) Sweet Salmon (HF) String cheese Greek Yogurt Laughing Cow cheese	Chicken Soup (HF) Lamb Ribs (HF) Chocolate Pudding (LF) Beef Skewers (HF) Sunflower seeds

2125 Kcal (67% fat)

Day 1	Day 2	Day 3	Day 4	Day 5	Day 6	Day 7
Italian Beef(HF) Beef Stew (HF) Egg Drop Soup (HF) Tuna can Sunflower seeds Laughing Cow cheese	Chicken Shawarma (LF) Stuffed Peppers (HF) Glazed Turkey (HF) Walnuts Boiled egg Tuna can	Masala Lamb (HF) Spicy Beef Soup (LF) Berry Slice (HF) Sweet Salmon (LF) Sunflower seeds Tuna can	Beef Skewers (HF) Sweet Salmon (HF) Chocolate Pudding (LF) Spicy Beef Soup (LF) Pork rinds String cheese	Italian Beef(HF) Beef Stew (HF) Egg Drop Soup (HF) Tuna can Sunflower seeds Laughing Cow cheese	Chicken Shawarma (LF) Stuffed Peppers (HF) Glazed Turkey (HF) Walnuts Boiled egg Tuna can	Masala Lamb (HF) Spicy Beef Soup (LF) Berry Slice (HF) Sweet Salmon (LF) Sunflower seeds Tuna can
Day 8	**Day 9**	**Day 10**	**Day 11**	**Day 12**	**Day 13**	**Day 14**
Beef Skewers (HF) Sweet Salmon (HF) Chocolate Pudding (LF) Spicy Beef Soup (LF) Pork rinds String cheese	Italian Beef(HF) Beef Stew (HF) Egg Drop Soup (HF) Tuna can Sunflower seeds Laughing Cow cheese	Masala Lamb (HF) Spicy Beef Soup (LF) Berry Slice (HF) Sweet Salmon (LF) Sunflower seeds Tuna can	Chicken Shawarma (LF) Stuffed Peppers (HF) Glazed Turkey (HF) Walnuts Boiled egg Tuna can	Beef Skewers (HF) Sweet Salmon (HF) Chocolate Pudding (LF) Spicy Beef Soup (LF) Pork rinds String cheese	Masala Lamb (HF) Spicy Beef Soup (LF) Berry Slice (HF) Sweet Salmon (LF) Sunflower seeds Tuna can	Beef Skewers (HF) Sweet Salmon (HF) Chocolate Pudding (LF) Spicy Beef Soup (LF) Pork rinds String cheese

2125 Kcal (75% fat)

Day 1	Day 2	Day 3	Day 4	Day 5	Day 6	Day 7
Chicken Shawarma (LF) Turkey Stir Fry (HF) Italian Beef (HF) Sunflower seeds Boiled egg	Chicken Cacciatore(HF) Turkey Stir Fry (LF) Chipotle Soup (HF) Spiced Pancakes (HF)	Herbed Pork Chops (HF) Masala Lamb (HF) Beef Skewers (HF) Chocolate Pudding (HF)	Lamb Skewers (HF) Beef Meatballs (HF) Turkey Thighs (HF) Peanut Cheesecake (HF) 4 egg whites	Chicken Shawarma (LF) Turkey Stir Fry (HF) Italian Beef (HF) Sunflower seeds Boiled egg	Chicken Cacciatore(HF) Turkey Stir Fry (LF) Chipotle Soup (HF) Spiced Pancakes (HF)	Herbed Pork Chops (HF) Masala Lamb (HF) Beef Skewers (HF) Chocolate Pudding (HF)
Day 8	**Day 9**	**Day 10**	**Day 11**	**Day 12**	**Day 13**	**Day 14**
Lamb Skewers (HF) Beef Meatballs (HF) Turkey Thighs (HF) Peanut Cheesecake (HF) 4 egg whites	Chicken Shawarma (LF) Turkey Stir Fry (LF) Italian Beef (HF) Sunflower seeds Boiled egg	Herbed Pork Chops (HF) Masala Lamb (HF) Beef Skewers (HF) Chocolate Pudding (HF)	Lamb Skewers (HF) Beef Meatballs (HF) Turkey Thighs (HF) Peanut Cheesecake (HF) 4 egg whites	Chicken Cacciatore(HF) Turkey Stir Fry (LF) Chipotle Soup (HF) Spiced Pancakes (HF)	Herbed Pork Chops (HF) Masala Lamb (HF) Beef Skewers (HF) Chocolate Pudding (HF)	Lamb Skewers (HF) Beef Meatballs (HF) Turkey Thighs (HF) Peanut Cheesecake (HF) 4 egg whites

2375 Kcal (73% fat)

Day 1	Day 2	Day 3	Day 4	Day 5	Day 6	Day 7
Chicken Hainanese (HF) Turkey Stir Fry (LF) Eggy Muffins (LF) Asparagus Soup (LF) Spiced Pancakes (HF) Pork rinds Laughing Cow cheese	Herbed Pork Chops (HF) Turkey Thighs (HF) Chocolate Pudding (HF) Beef Skewers (HF) Peanut Cheesecake (LF) Laughing Cow cheese 1 egg white	Stuffed Chicken (LF) Egg Frittata (HF) Eggy Muffins (HF) Stuffed Chicken (HF) Sunflower seeds Jerky	Lamb Skewers (HF) Tandoori chicken (LF) Berry Slice (LF) Lamb Ribs (HF) Chocolate Pudding (LF) Walnuts	Chicken Hainanese (HF) Turkey Stir Fry (LF) Eggy Muffins (LF) Asparagus Soup (LF) Spiced Pancakes (HF) Pork rinds Laughing Cow cheese	Herbed Pork Chops (HF) Turkey Thighs (HF) Chocolate Pudding (HF) Beef Skewers (HF) Peanut Cheesecake (LF) Laughing Cow cheese 1 egg white	Lamb Skewers (HF) Tandoori chicken (LF) Berry Slice (LF) Lamb Ribs (HF) Chocolate Pudding (LF) Walnuts
Day 8	**Day 9**	**Day 10**	**Day 11**	**Day 12**	**Day 13**	**Day 14**
Stuffed Chicken (LF) Egg Frittata (HF) Eggy Muffins (HF) Stuffed Chicken (HF) Sunflower seeds Jerky	Herbed Pork Chops (HF) Turkey Thighs (HF) Chocolate Pudding (HF) Beef Skewers (HF) Peanut Cheesecake (LF) Laughing Cow cheese 1 egg white	Lamb Skewers (HF) Tandoori chicken (LF) Berry Slice (LF) Lamb Ribs (HF) Chocolate Pudding (LF) Walnuts	Chicken Hainanese (HF) Turkey Stir Fry (LF) Eggy Muffins (LF) Asparagus Soup (LF) Spiced Pancakes (HF) Pork rinds Laughing Cow cheese	Herbed Pork Chops (HF) Turkey Thighs (HF) Chocolate Pudding (HF) Beef Skewers (HF) Peanut Cheesecake (LF) Laughing Cow cheese 1 egg white	Stuffed Chicken (LF) Egg Frittata (HF) Eggy Muffins (HF) Stuffed Chicken (HF) Sunflower seeds Jerky	Lamb Skewers (HF) Tandoori chicken (LF) Berry Slice (LF) Lamb Ribs (HF) Chocolate Pudding (LF) Walnuts

Meal Plans